13 STEPS TO BLOODY GOOD SALES

ASHWIN SANGHI
ANAND PRAKASH
ROHIT GOEL

13 STEPS TO BLOODY GOOD SALES

Published by Westland Books, a division of Nasadiya Technologies Private Limited, in 2025

No. 269/2B, First Floor, 'Irai Arul', Vimalraj Street, Nethaji Nagar, Alapakkam Main Road, Maduravoyal, Chennai 600095

Westland and the Westland logo are the trademarks of Nasadiya Technologies Private Limited, or its affiliates.

Copyright © Ashwin Sanghi, 2025

Ashwin Sanghi asserts the moral right to be identified as the author of this work.

ISBN: 9789371974158

10 9 8 7 6 5 4 3 2 1

The views and opinions expressed in this work are the author's own and the facts are as reported by him, and the publisher is in no way liable for the same.

All rights reserved

Typeset by Jojy Philip

Printed at Manipal Technologies Limited, Manipal

No part of this book may be reproduced, or stored in a retrieval system, or transmitted in any form or by any means, electronic, mechanical, photocopying, recording, or otherwise, without express written permission of the publisher.

CONTENTS

About the Authors — vii
Foreword — xi
Introduction — xiii

STEP ONE: Sharpen Your Product Knowledge — 1
STEP TWO: Perfect Your Prospecting — 22
STEP THREE: Refine Your Pitch — 37
STEP FOUR: Optimise the Funnel — 56
STEP FIVE: Manage Your Time — 75
STEP SIX: Master the Close — 87
STEP SEVEN: Stay Organised — 102
STEP EIGHT: Nurture Your Relationships — 119
STEP NINE: Develop a 24x7 Mindset — 138
STEP TEN: Invest in You — 157
STEP ELEVEN: Leverage the Crisis — 174
STEP TWELVE: Build Your Personal Brand — 187
STEP THIRTEEN: Embrace Continuous Growth — 198
STEP FOURTEEN: Determine Your Fit — 210

ABOUT THE AUTHORS

Ashwin Sanghi is among India's highest-selling English fiction authors. His bestselling Bharat Collection includes *The Rozabal Line, Chanakya's Chant, The Krishna Key, The Sialkot Saga, Keepers of the Kalachakra, The Vault of Vishnu, The Magicians of Mazda* and *The Ayodhya Alliance*. He has also co-authored two *New York Times* bestsellers—*Private India* and *Private Delhi*—with James Patterson. Ashwin co-writes and edits the top-rated *13 Steps* self-help series (on luck, wealth, health, marks, parenting—and now sales), and the *Kutta Kadam* crime thriller series. A regular contributor to the *Times of India* op-ed pages, he has been featured in *Forbes India's* Celebrity 100 and the *New Indian Express's* Culture Power List. His many honours include the Crossword Popular Choice Award (2012), Atta Galatta Award (2018), WBR Iconic Achievers Award (2018), Lit-O-Fest Literature Legend Award (2018), Kalinga Popular Choice Award (2021) and the Deendayal Upadhyaya Recognition (2023). Ashwin studied at the Cathedral and John Connon School and St. Xavier's College in Mumbai, holds an MBA from Yale University and a DLitt (Honoris Causa) from JECRC University. Connect with Ashwin: Email ashwinsanghioffice@gmail.com | Website: www.

sanghi.in | Facebook: @ashwinsanghi | X: @ashwinsanghi | YouTube: /ashwinsanghi | Instagram: @ashwin.sanghi | LinkedIn: /in/ashwinsanghi

Anand Prakash is a serial entrepreneur and seasoned leader with over twenty-five years in the automotive industry. He is the co-founder and managing director of Performance Cars Private Limited, which operates the BMW Infinity Cars dealership in Delhi, renowned for its customer excellence. His journey began with impactful roles at Honda Motorcycles & Scooters and Maruti Suzuki India. A gold medallist in mechanical engineering and an MBA in sales and marketing, Anand blends technical expertise with strategic insight. He was named Entrepreneur of the Year 2023 by *The Economic Times* and serves as the regional director at Federation of Automobile Dealers Associations (FADA), influencing national industry policy. Anand is also a respected consultant, motivational speaker and management coach, committed to mentoring and giving back through active NGO involvement. Connect with Anand: Email: andyps2006@gmail.com | Facebook: @anandprakash | Instagram: @anandprakash461 | LinkedIn: /in/anand-prakash

Rohit Goel is the bestselling author of *Fall, Don't Fail* (2021) and a poetry book titled *Maa* (2025). He is a transformative leader with over twenty-five years in senior roles across organisations like Birla Cement, General Motors, Maruti Suzuki and Bajaj Auto. Known for his 'industry-first' leadership models and human-centric approach, Rohit is a strategist, mentor and storyteller. His debut book, inspired by real-life events, became a two-time Amazon bestseller. Beyond the boardroom, he is a certified laughter yoga facilitator and founder of Laugh Every Day—Nirvana, a club promoting joy and well-being. A BTech graduate and MBA gold medallist, he is a fitness enthusiast, experimental cook and writer currently working on new titles in poetry, leadership and short fiction. Rohit believes in giving back to society by volunteering at many forums, including road safety and uplifting underprivileged children by way of education. Connect with Rohit: Email: roship2001@gmail.com | X: @roship2001 | YouTube: /rojagoel | Instagram: @rohitgoel_author | LinkedIn: /in/rohitgoel0701| Website: www.rohitgoel.co.in

FOREWORD

The *13 Steps* series has always been a labour of love—my way of untangling life's chaos into something clear, doable and (hopefully) helpful. From luck to wealth, health and academics to parenting—and now, sales—my co-authors and I have explored themes that shape us. And every book has shaped us right back.

When Anand and Rohit pitched the idea of writing *13 Steps to Bloody Good Sales*, I was instantly hooked. Not just because sales is everywhere (it is), but because it's misunderstood—often reduced to 'slick talk' or pushy pitches. In truth, sales is about trust, empathy, grit and timing. It's equal parts art and psychology. And, if you ask me, it's one of the most valuable life skills out there.

Before I became a storyteller seventeen years ago, I ran businesses in multiple sectors ranging from manufacturing to automobiles to real estate and e-commerce. So, I've seen first-hand how powerful great salesmanship can be—and how rare it is. That's why I was excited when Anand and Rohit, two genuine masters of the game, decided to bottle their decades of sales wisdom into one smart, story-filled guide.

Because let's be honest: we're all in sales. Whether you're convincing a client to approve a design, a colleague to adopt a new process or your five-year-old to eat broccoli—it's all selling. Yet, few of us are taught how to do it well. That's where this book comes in.

As Robert Louis Stevenson once said, 'Everyone lives by selling something.' Whether you're pitching an idea, a dream or the last slice of pizza—it's all sales. But here's the twist: great salespeople aren't born; they're self-made. With the right tools, habits and mindset, anyone can sell. Anand and Rohit are living proof.

What you're holding is more than a book. It's a hands-on field guide. Part manual, part motivator. It's packed with practical steps, real stories and just the right amount of kick-in-the-pants encouragement to help you thrive in sales—whether you're starting out or levelling up.

Anand and Rohit brought the hard-earned wisdom; I just spiced up the storytelling. Together, I think we've created something useful, fun and (dare I say) bloody brilliant.

Welcome to the game.

Ashwin Sanghi
Mumbai, 2025

INTRODUCTION

Hello, dear reader—and welcome!

We're thrilled you picked up *13 Steps to Bloody Good Sales* because this book is as much about real life as it is about closing deals. Before we get into the meat of the book, let's rewind to a breezy evening in Mumbai, where this whole project began.

Picture this: three guys—Ashwin, Rohit and Anand (that's me)—parked at a seaside café, sipping single malts and watching the sun do its dramatic dip into the Arabian Sea. Somewhere between the second drink and the fourth round of banter, Ashwin asked a question that changed our plans for the near future: 'We've spent decades in sales ... but what have we *really* given back to the profession that made us?'

Now, Ashwin isn't just a bestselling author; he's managed businesses across automobiles, real estate, exports and e-commerce before he transitioned to the literary world. His mind is always working, always connecting dots. 'Sure, we've trained teams, spoken at B-schools,' he said, 'but isn't that still small-scale? What if we could reach *thousands* ... maybe *millions*?'

Rohit jumped in. 'I've trained sales professionals, spoken at corporate events, mentored students. I've sold everything from sedans to software to seeds. I even wrote a corporate bestseller!' he offered.

Not good enough, said Ashwin's grin. 'A few hundred people? Come on. Let's go bigger.'

That's when I raised my glass. 'Alright then, here's my two cents,' I said. 'I started off selling copper scrap. Then it was nuts and bolts. Then bikes and cars for Honda and Maruti Suzuki. Now I run a BMW dealership in Delhi. I train my teams, lecture at colleges and advise companies. And yes, I've got a lot of stories.'

Ashwin leaned in. 'Great. Now can we turn those stories into a book?'

And then we brought up Farrokh Bhoot, the legendary salesperson at Ashwin's ancestral auto business. If anyone ever made selling look like magic, it was Farrokh. He had charm, heart, memory like a steel trap and the rare ability to make customers feel like family. 'What if we could create more Farrokhs?' we asked. *Boom. That was it. The spark. The idea.*

We began pooling everything we knew—our lessons, stumbles, wild wins and forehead-slap fails. We weren't just writing a book; we were crafting a field manual for anyone who wants to *sell smart, sell ethically and sell like a rockstar*.

So, yes, this book is about selling. But, it's also about connection, trust, self-awareness, creativity and grit.

Whether you're a rookie or a rainmaker, the thirteen steps we share here will help you sharpen your game and walk into any sales scenario with clarity and confidence.

Because sales isn't about tricking people. It's about *understanding* them. As John Maxwell said, 'People don't buy because they understand you. They buy because you understand them.'

Let's get started.

Anand Prakash and Rohit Goel
New Delhi, 2025

STEP 1: SHARPEN YOUR PRODUCT KNOWLEDGE

Let me begin with a confession: my first real sales pitch was an absolute disaster.

Picture this: twenty-two-year-old Anand Prakash, fresh out of engineering college, nervously clutching a battered briefcase filled with copper scrap samples. The customer leaned back in his chair and asked, 'What's the copper purity percentage of this lot?'

I blinked. I stammered. Honestly, in that moment, I couldn't even have told you the purity of the chai I drank that morning. Needless to say, the client politely showed me the door.

That day, I learnt my first brutal lesson in sales: if you don't know your product, you don't deserve the customer's money.

And, trust me, customers can smell inexperience the way we Indians smell ghee in a kitchen two floors down.

Why Is Product Knowledge Non-Negotiable?

Over the years, from selling nuts and bolts, to leading Maruti Suzuki teams, to now running my own BMW dealerships, one truth has stayed consistent: product knowledge is your superpower.

If you know your product inside out, you sell with authority, with confidence, with swagger. But if you don't? Well, you'll be selling like you're reading off a teleprompter at a spelling bee.

Think of it like this: would you trust a pilot who says, 'I think this button flies the plane?' Or a chef who doesn't know what spices went into your butter chicken? No way!

Starting a sales journey without knowing your product is like heading on a road trip without a map—you'll struggle to reach the destination.

Now imagine this: you're a customer having conversations with two reps for the same product. One of them can answer all your questions and even offers tips on using the product better. The other fumbles and checks his phone for answers. Who do you trust more? Exactly. That's the power of product knowledge.

I often tell my sales teams: the more you know, the less you have to sell. It's almost as though customers convince themselves.

Customers will sometimes quiz you with the sole intention of checking whether you really know your product. It is almost like they are daring you to a duel. It is your preparation that will decide who wins.

Jeffrey Gitomer, an American author and speaker who writes and lectures on sales, famously says, 'In the world of sales, the more you know, the more you sell.'

The funny thing is that sales isn't about dazzling people with fancy features, it's about making them feel as if they're making an informed, brilliant decision. (Even if that brilliant decision costs them ₹1 crore and their right kidney.)

When Steve Jobs was launching the first iPhone, he famously rehearsed the demo for each and every feature dozens of times to ensure he could explain it without a hitch. His deep knowledge of the product made his presentations legendary.

It is often joked—and rightly so—that if you don't know your product like the back of your hand, you'll end up selling by the seat of your pants.

How to Build Bloody Good Product Knowledge the SMART Way

OK, now you're convinced product knowledge is critical. But you're probably thinking: 'Sounds great, Anand ... but how do I actually build it?'

Don't worry. I'm not about to throw some boring MBA jargon at you. (I suffered enough during my own MBA programme. No need to inflict that trauma on you.)

Instead, let's keep it simple with a formula I use even today: SMART. It stands for: Sessions, Manuals, Application, Reviews and Trends. Let's break it down, the Anand way.

Sessions (aka Get Schooled)

Early in my Maruti Suzuki days, I attended a technical training session for one of the new car models. The instructor spent what felt like an eternity talking about things like 'chassis

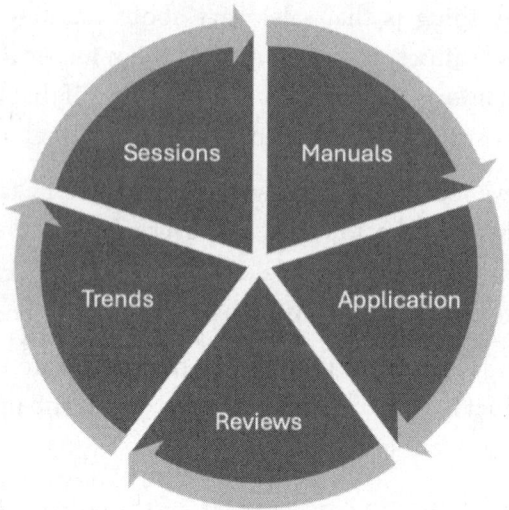

rigidity' and 'body torsional strength'—stuff that sounded impressive but made half the room quietly wish for samosas instead.

I stayed awake, more out of survival instinct than curiosity, fuelled by three cups of machine coffee. (Terrible coffee, but when you're new in sales, survival > taste.)

A few days later, a serious-looking fleet customer—an engineer, no less—walked into our corporate office. After reviewing the specs, he casually asked, 'How does the new model's body rigidity compare to the earlier one? I heard it affects handling and NVH levels.'

Boom. That coffee-fuelled lecture flashed back into my head.

Because I had actually paid attention, I could explain how the stiffer chassis improved cornering stability and reduced cabin noise. And just like that, I earned his trust.

Lesson learnt: training sessions may feel boring while you're sitting in them, but, trust me, they're like invisible armour. You only realise their value when you're standing in front of a customer who knows more about cars than your whole WhatsApp group combined. A great sales professional never misses a chance to attend training programmes.

Manuals (The Secret Superpower You're Ignoring)
Frankly, the only manual I had ever read properly before joining Honda was for my college bike; and even that, only because I wanted to figure out how to reset the trip meter before a road trip.

In the real world of sales, though, I quickly realised something: the product manual isn't just a boring book; it's your secret weapon. It's your Gita, Bible, Quran—and if you're a Marvel fan like me, your origin story rolled into one.

In the early days, I'd fumble when customers asked about feature details. I'd bluff, dodge, smile awkwardly—basically, everything except answer properly.

Until one night, frustrated with myself, I stayed back after work, picked up the latest model brochure and actually started reading it like a novel. And guess what? The more I understood—the real killer features, the little technical specs customers love to quote, the answers to their most common questions—the more my confidence skyrocketed.

A common mistake salespeople make is to look at the product manual only when they get free time—which is never! You have to make time to learn. It will pay you rich dividends.

Cheat tip: whenever you read a manual or brochure, focus on three things:

- *Killer features*: What's truly unique about this product?
- *Technical specs*: The shiny numbers customers admire (and use to impress their friends).
- *Common FAQs*: The questions that always pop up during a demo—have your answers ready.

When I started selling BMWs, this habit paid off in spades. I could rattle off details like 'torque vectoring on an xDrive system' without blinking. One evening, I casually dropped it into a customer conversation, and the gentleman was so impressed he insisted on bringing his wife for a second visit. (Meanwhile, my own wife thought I was either possessed or talking in code.)

Moral of the story: the manual may look boring, but inside it lies the ammunition you'll need to win the battlefield called 'customer conversation'.

Application (Use It or Lose It)

If you really want to understand your product—I mean *really* understand it—you need to use it, live with it, breathe it.

When we first got a BMW model equipped with gesture control—where you could wave your hand to change the music volume or answer calls—I remember spending hours in the demo car practising it. Waving left, waving right, adjusting the angle, checking the speed of response ... you get the drift. It felt silly at first, but soon I became the go-to person whenever a customer wanted a live demonstration.

And let me tell you, it made all the difference. Instead of just telling customers about the feature, I could show them exactly how it worked:

- Which gestures were the smoothest
- How quick the response was
- What the quirks were.

Bottom line: don't just talk about your product like a brochure on legs; experience it yourself. Drive it. Press every button. Test every feature.

- If it's a car, live in it for a day.
- If it's a phone, use all its features.
- If it's a camera, shoot several photos.
- If it's a mattress, lie on it (following hygiene protocols, of course!).

To sell well, experience the product. If you're promoting a new treadmill, run on it yourself. Familiarise yourself with its settings, track how smoothly it runs, see what valuable information it displays and understand the feel of its impact on your joints. Your personal experience with it allows you to describe not just its features but how it *feels*. You'll be able to help customers imagine it in their own home gyms.

Because customers can sense it instantly when you speak from real experience, not a memorised script. When you've used the product, it transforms the way you communicate with the potential buyer: your body language is confident, your passion appears genuine and your sales pitch sounds natural.

Reviews (The Gossip Columns of Sales)

I have another confession to make: I spend more time reading customer reviews on Google, Reddit and in *Autocar* than following news about what happens in Parliament. Why? Because reviews on the web, social media, Amazon, Quora and other platforms tell you what users love, hate and wish for. They teach you the language of the customer.

I came across a hilarious review online, which read: 'This car accelerates faster than my mother-in-law's judgement.' (I instantly stole that line for my next sales pitch.)

Also, keep an eye on competitor reviews. Know what customers are cribbing about in rival products, so you can *subtly* highlight how your offering is better. (Subtly, my friends. We're salespeople, not Bollywood villains.)

It's not enough to know what your company says about your product; you must also know what the market says about it. It makes your pitch richer and more credible.

Trends (Stay Updated or Get Outdated)

I follow product updates and industry gossip like people follow IPL scores. New features, regulatory changes, customer preferences—they all change faster than Delhi weather.

When electric vehicles (EVs) started becoming hot, half my sales guys still thought that Tesla was a new energy drink. *Don't be that guy.*

Subscribe to trade magazines, follow relevant blogs and attend company events, webinars and networking sessions. Tracking consumer behaviour analytics and social media buzz around your product. Essentially, stay ahead. This will immensely help you to craft relatable pitches.

Just like software, your knowledge needs regular updates to stay relevant. If a customer knows more than you, you've already lost half the battle. Remember: in today's world, if you are not updated, you are outdated.

Quick Recap of SMART

Element	Why It Matters	Anand's Tip
Sessions	Learn from the pros	Stay caffeinated
Manuals	Know every key feature	Use cheat sheets
Application	Personal experience sells	Play like a kid
Reviews	Speak customer language	Borrow good lines
Trends	Stay current	Read more, scroll less

A great salesman once quipped, 'Product knowledge is like innerwear: essential, but not meant to be shown off. Give just enough for the customer to feel comfortable.' I couldn't have put it better myself.

Turn Your Knowledge into Magic: The FAB Way

All right, now you're a walking encyclopaedia of your product. But here's the big question: how do you translate all that knowledge into something the customer actually cares about?

Enter another of my favourite frameworks: FAB. It stands for Features, Advantages and Benefits. I call it the 'Samosa Principle' of selling.

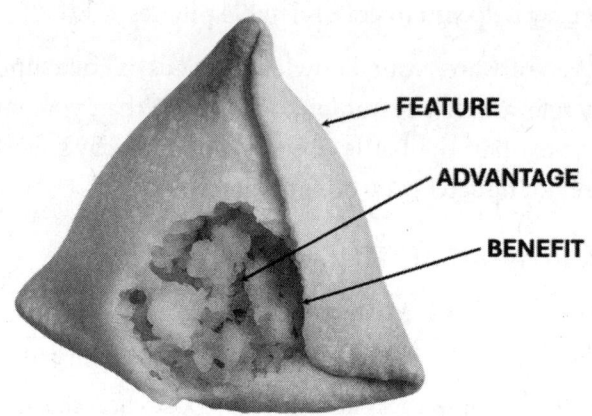

- The **feature** is the golden crispy layer outside.
- The **advantage** is the hot and spicy aloo filling inside.
- And the **benefit** is that first bite when you feel pure happiness flood your soul.

If you just show the crispy outside (feature) without telling them there's spicy potato inside (advantage) or why it matters (benefit), people might just walk away.

How FAB Saved a Deal (True Story!)

One afternoon at our BMW dealership, one of my newer sales executives was handling a customer inquiry about the 3 Series Gran Limousine.

Now, this young man was fresh out of training and feeling very proud of his technical knowledge. So, he began pitching like a machine gun:

'Sir, it's got a 2.0L TwinPower Turbo engine, 258 bhp and a rear seat longer by 110 mm.' The customer listened politely and then excused himself, saying he had 'another appointment'.

No follow-up. No deal.

When the executive came back looking deflated, we sat down for a quick review. I asked him: 'Did you talk about how the car would make the customer feel? Or were you just throwing numbers at him?'

That's when it clicked for him. He realised he had been stuck at features, without translating them into benefits that mattered to the customer. What he should have said was something like: 'Sir, the 3 Series Limousine offers the perfect balance—the sporty thrill you expect when you're driving alone and the luxurious space to stretch out after a long day at work. It's like owning a racehorse that also knows how to give you a massage.'

(Guess who corrected his pitch the next day ... and closed a sale to a similar customer!)

Break it down like this:

- *Feature* = What it is
  (Turbo engine, extended rear seat, 10.25" touchscreen)
- *Advantage* = What it does better
  (More power, more legroom, better infotainment)

- *Benefit* = Why should the customer care
  (Feel exhilarated on your drive, relax like royalty, impress friends without saying a word)

Always complete the cycle:

$$\text{Feature} \to \text{Advantage} \to \text{Benefit}.$$

Never leave a customer halfway up the hill.

Some Quick FAB Examples

Product	Feature	Advantage	Benefit
BMW xDrive	All-wheel drive system	Better grip and control	Drive safely even during the monsoon—no slipping, no skidding
iPhone 15	Ceramic shield glass	4x better drop resistance	Your screen survives your butterfinger moments
Luxury mattress	Memory foam	Adjusts to body shape	Sleep like a king, wake up without back pain
Water purifier	Multi-stage filtration	Removes bacteria, viruses, metals	Keep your family healthy, one sip at a time

Storytelling Sells the Benefit

Imagine you're selling handcrafted jewellery from Rajasthan—each piece is an intricate work of art, carefully crafted by hand and telling a story of tradition, skill and time. When customers hear that story, they feel they're not just buying jewellery but becoming part of a cultural legacy.

Or consider an eco-friendly sneaker brand made from recycled materials. Customers aren't just buying these shoes, they're buying into sustainability, making a statement about their values.

Or a luxury watch like a Rolex or Piaget that doesn't just tell time—it signals achievement.

Remember, FAB is more than facts. It's about feeling, aspiration and identity.

Anand's Cheat Tip: Master the 'So What?' Game

Whenever you're explaining anything to a customer, just remember the magic words: 'So what?' After every point you make, pretend the customer is asking you, 'So what?' Your job is to answer it clearly.

'It has an advanced engine.'

So what?

'It accelerates faster and drives smoother.'

So what?

'You'll enjoy every road trip and beat city traffic without breaking a sweat.'

That's the gold. If you can't answer the 'So what?' clearly, you haven't gone deep enough into FAB.

Know Your Customer's Heart (and Head): The ERF Formula

Now you know how to explain your product beautifully using FAB. But here's something else I have learnt after years of selling from scrap, nuts, bikes and cars: not every customer is driven by logic.

Some buy with their heart, some with their brain and some with their wallet. To win, you need to understand who's in the driving seat—*emotion, reason* or *practicality*. That's where ERF comes in.

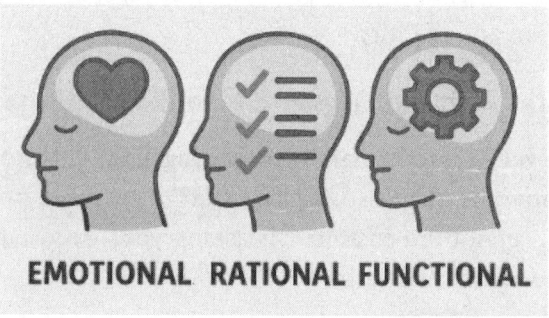

If you can figure out whether the customer is thinking emotionally, rationally or functionally, you can pitch perfectly.

Emotional Customers (Dilwale Customers)

These customers buy because the product makes them feel good.

One day, a very dear friend who is a Padma Shri-awardee doctor visited me at my BMW showroom. He was nattily dressed in his custom-tailored suit and had a cigar in his hand. There was a BMW Z4 convertible on display, and he fell in love with the car at first sight. He sat in the car in utter silence like a kid with a twinkle in his eyes.

Finally, he said, 'Anand, the moment I sat in this car, I felt like Shah Rukh Khan.'

Deal closed. (He has even named his car Zizu and treats it like a baby.)

Lesson learnt:

When you're selling to emotional buyers, don't talk specs. Talk feelings, dreams, status, pride, romance. Make them imagine how wonderful their life will be with your product.

Sample lines for emotional customers:

- 'Imagine the look on your friends' faces when you drive in.'
- 'This car isn't just fast; it announces you've arrived.'
- 'It's not just a mattress. It's your private island after a hard day.'

Rational Customers (Dimaagwale Customers)

Now, some customers approach buying like they're preparing for the UPSC exam.

These folks want spreadsheets, comparisons, data points, safety ratings, warranty details, resale values (basically, the very opposite of emotional buyers).

I once spent two hours with a software engineer explaining how Maruti's maintenance packages compared to Hyundai's and Tata's. We both nearly needed a doctor by the end of it. But, hey, he bought it. Because I fed his brain exactly what it wanted: hard facts.

A business selecting a software solution cares less about a flashy interface and more about uptime, integration capabilities and support responsiveness.

Lesson learnt:

When it comes to rational buyers:

- Be detailed.
- Be logical.
- Be ready with third-party proofs and numbers.
- Never fake anything—you'll be caught instantly.

Sample lines for rational customers:

- 'Our car has the highest crash-test rating in its class.'
- 'Studies show this appliance reduces electricity bills by 12 per cent annually.'
- 'Compared to competitors, our insurance plan offers double the coverage for the same premium.'

Functional Customers (Jugaadwale Customers)

And then there's the largest group: functional buyers.

They're not swayed by brand ambassadors or glossy TV ads. They don't care if their microwave looks like it belongs in a space station. They want value. Simplicity. Durability.

A saleswoman I know, Priya, was once enthusiastically pitching a high-end, smart microwave oven with voice commands and Wi-Fi control. She was halfway through explaining how it could sync with a smartphone when the customer—a middle-aged, no-nonsense lady—cut her off and said: *'Beta, bas yeh bata do, dahi jamtaa hai ya nahin iss mein?'* Will it set curd properly or not? Priorities!

Lesson learnt:

Functional buyers care about real-life utility, not futuristic fluff. You could offer them a flying fridge, but if it doesn't keep bhindi fresh for three days, they're not buying it.

Sample lines for functional customers:

- 'You won't have to worry about water purifier maintenance—we offer doorstep service, even in smaller towns.'
- 'This phone's battery lasts two days on a single charge—you won't be hunting for a charger at noon.'
- 'It folds flat in the boot—you'll never struggle with loading luggage again.'

Anand's Quick Tip: Play Customer Detective

When the customer walks in, ask yourself quietly: 'Is this person buying for feelings, for logic or for function?'

Then adapt your pitch accordingly. Sometimes you'll even meet a customer who is part emotional, part rational. And this is when selling becomes masala Bollywood—you throw in a little emotion, a little logic and seal the deal.

Real-Life Example: One Family, Three Buyers

During my time at Maruti Suzuki, Sandeep, a team leader at one of the dealerships in my region, shared an interesting story that made me smile.

'Sir,' he said, 'yesterday I handled a classic Indian family buying moment.'

A family had walked into the showroom looking at a Maruti Dzire—a practical sedan for city and family use. As Sandeep started showing them around the car, he quickly realised he wasn't selling to just one buyer. He was dealing with three very different personalities.

- The son, just starting his career, was excited about the car's sporty looks. 'It looks so cool with the alloys, Dad!' (Emotional buyer)
- The father, a cautious, calculator-carrying gentleman, immediately asked about mileage, insurance costs and resale value. (Rational buyer)
- The mother, after walking around the car, quietly asked: 'Beta, will I be able to get in and out easily? My knees aren't what they used to be.' (Functional buyer)

Sandeep managed to adjust his pitch on the spot:

- For the son, he highlighted the stylish dual-tone interiors and sleek design.
- For the father, he shared the Dzire's fuel efficiency figures, low maintenance costs and strong resale reputation.

- And for the mother, he demonstrated the wide door opening, higher seating position and soft-touch seat cushioning for easier entry and exit.

They didn't book the car immediately—but returned three days later, this time much more relaxed. And guess what, they signed the booking form!

The lesson Sandeep shared with me (and I've repeated this to many teams since): 'If you just focus on features without understanding their real concerns, you lose the sale. If you pitch to their hearts and heads together—you win.'

Understanding whether someone is guided by their heart, head or habit while buying is what separates a good salesperson from a bloody good one.

Quick Cheat Sheet

Customer Type	Focus On	Avoid
Emotional	Feelings, lifestyle, status	Too much tech jargon
Rational	Data, proof, comparisons	Overhyping emotions
Functional	Practical benefits, ease, cost	Fancy luxuries they didn't ask for

Wrapping Up

If you've stayed with me through all the stories, jokes and samosa analogies, here's the honest truth I want to leave you with: product knowledge is not a 'nice-to-have'. It's a 'need-to-survive'.

Without it, you're a street magician pulling rabbits out of a hat. With it, you're a seasoned chef serving Michelin-star dishes. Big difference, my friend!

And remember: product knowledge isn't about stuffing your brain with 5,000 bullet points. It's about understanding how your product fits into your customer's life.

- When you know it, you speak with confidence.
- When you don't, you speak with excuses.

Trust me, I've been that nervous, clueless kid, and I've also been the confident guy closing multi-crore deals. Product knowledge was the bridge between the two.

Anand's Final Five Tips to Remember

- *Dive deep:* Don't settle for knowing surface-level facts. Know the why behind every what.
- *Use SMART:* Attend Sessions. Read Manuals. Apply the Product. Study Reviews. Track Trends.
- *Master FAB:* Show the Feature → Explain the Advantage → Make them feel the Benefit.
- *Decipher ERF:* Spot if the customer is Emotional, Rational or Functional—and pitch accordingly.
- *Keep evolving:* Today's perfect pitch is tomorrow's outdated joke. Keep learning. Stay hungry.

My Final Anecdote: The Chaiwala's Secret

There's a chaiwala near my farmhouse in Alwar. Nothing fancy—just a cart, a kettle and a never-ending queue of loyal customers.

One day, I asked him, 'Bhaiya, everyone sells chai. What's your secret?'

He smiled and said: 'Simple, sahab. *Har aadmi ko uske mood ke hisaab se chai milti hai. Kisi ko kadak, kisi ko meethi, kisi ko adrak wali, kisi ko halki.*' Simple, sir. Everyone gets the tea that matches their mood—strong, sweet, gingery or light.

And just like that, it clicked.

He wasn't just selling tea. He was observing people, remembering preferences and adapting the same product to suit different needs. Now that is a bloody good salesperson— not pushing what you want to sell, but matching what they actually need at that moment.

Know your product. Know your customer. And serve the perfect cup of chai. Whether you're selling cars, copper scrap, tea or cupcakes, the principle stays the same, *Know. Connect. Convert.*

STEP 2: PERFECT YOUR PROSPECTING

I have a massive confession to make: I wasn't always great at finding customers. Picture this: Rohit Goel (that's me), fresh MBA gold medal in hand, newly minted and full of confidence. My first assignment? Selling Xerox photocopiers across Delhi. I showed up early, stood proud outside our showroom, brochures in hand, tie in place, believing customers would walk in just because I was ready.

Day after day, I polished machines, aligned flyers, waited by the door and told myself I was being patient. Until one day, my regional head dropped by. He saw my set-up, nodded, then gently put a hand on my shoulder and said, 'Goel, you've got the right energy, but in sales, we don't wait for the rain. We fetch buckets and make it happen.'

That one sentence shifted something in me and I learnt my second and most humbling lesson in sales: *if you're not actively finding your customers, you can't expect them to find you.*

So I closed the showroom binder, picked up my sample kit and stepped out into the streets—where real sales are made. Cold visits, copier demos in dusty offices, conversations with admin heads at tea stalls—that's where I started becoming a salesperson.

Finding Your Perfect Match

Have you ever been to a wedding and spotted that one uncle scanning the crowd like he's on a mission to find the perfect match for his son or daughter? Imagine him tossing flower petals everywhere, hoping to hit that one perfect person by chance. Not exactly efficient, right?

Now recall those classic Shaadi.com ads. The bride's father is going around trying to find a match—ready to put a sehra on any guy he sees. The ad then shows him creating a detailed profile on the matchmaking site based on his daughter's traits. The site delivers a list of prospective matches, and a happy wedding follows.

That, my friends, is what prospecting is all about: knowing your product inside out and finding the perfect 'match' for it. Think of it as fishing with a spear rather than casting an ultrawide net.

During my years at some of the country's largest automakers, I discovered that precision always beats volume. Advertising guru David Ogilvy rightly said, 'Don't count the people you reach; reach the people who count.' Real prospecting is targeted and strategic.

What Is Prospecting, Anyway?

Simply put, prospecting means identifying potential customers who have both *intent* (need, desire, willingness) and *content* (ability and authority) to buy what you're selling.

Jim Rohn, an American entrepreneur and motivational speaker, wrote, 'To succeed in sales, simply talk to lots of people every day. And here's what's exciting—there are lots of people.'

But not just any people—the *right* people.

Prospecting is the lifeline of your sales journey. If you're not constantly finding new customers, sales will dry up faster than a puddle in the Thar desert.

Finding Your Ideal Customer: The 4P Framework

When I first started, I would talk to anyone who'd listen. The results? Mediocre at best. It wasn't until I learnt to target the right customers that things changed.

To identify prospects, I use what I call the 4P framework: Place, Problem, Price, Power.

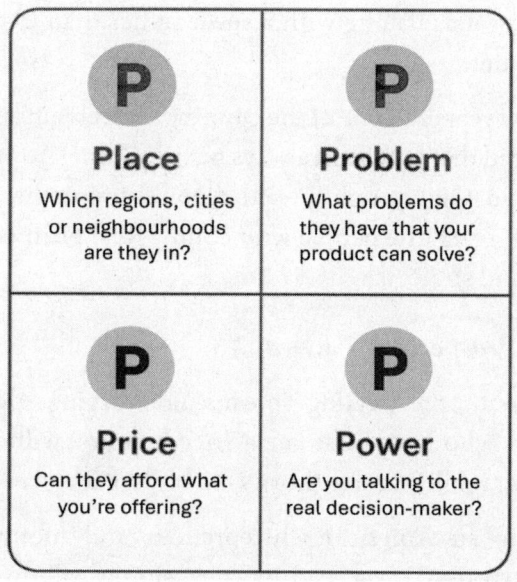

Place

Which regions, cities or localities are they in? Where are your customers located? Location affects needs and purchasing decisions. A salesperson selling monsoon gear should focus on regions with heavy rainfall like Meghalaya, not Rajasthan. A friend who was selling premium office furniture in Mumbai, focused on business districts like Nariman Point and Bandra–Kurla Complex.

Problem

What problems do they have that your product can solve? Identify the key issues, frustrations or aspirations your customers are dealing with. If you're selling water purifiers, the customer's 'problem' might be hard water damaging their appliances or health concerns about contamination.

Price

Can they afford what you're offering? It's not enough for them to want the product—they must be able to pay for it comfortably. If you're selling weekend homes, you're not targeting everyone—you're focusing on buyers with a high enough income or access to easy financing.

Power

Are you talking to the real decision-maker? Always check if the person you're speaking with has the authority to say 'yes'. If you're selling software to a company, the user might love it, but it's the finance head or CEO who signs the cheque. Sell to the one who holds the power.

The Story of Two Approaches

When I was the national head of sales at Bajaj Auto, I often worked closely with dealership teams across the country. I still remember two young hires at a Pune dealership who taught me a powerful lesson about prospecting.

Vikram was fresh out of college and full of energy. He decided that the best way to sell was to reach as many people as possible. He messaged almost everyone he knew about our new premium motorcycle—friends, acquaintances, even distant relatives. His approach was simple: cast a wide net and hope for the best. After a month of trying, he had managed a few polite conversations and a couple of test rides, but no actual sales.

Meanwhile, Sameer, another new recruit, took a very different route. He spent time studying who typically bought this kind of bike. He realised that it appealed most to young professionals in their late twenties to early forties—men who loved adventure, appreciated cutting-edge technology and had the financial stability to buy a premium motorcycle. Many of them were working in tech companies, running start-ups or climbing the ladder in corporate jobs, earning around ₹8 to ₹12 lakh a year.

Instead of messaging everyone blindly, Sameer focused on places where these riders naturally gathered. He started frequenting cafés near tech parks, connected with biking communities online and even joined a couple of weekend group rides. He didn't push the product immediately. Instead, he built conversations around biking adventures, technology and riding gear. Gradually, he built relationships and trust.

By the end of his second month, Sameer had closed two sales and had several more prospects seriously interested. The difference was obvious. While Vikram tried speaking to everyone, Sameer made sure he was speaking to the right people.

Effective Ways to Connect with Prospects

Once you've identified your ideal customer, it's time to connect. As motivational speaker Brian Tracy said, 'Keep your sales pipeline full by prospecting continuously. Always have more people to see than you have time to see them.'

Here are the most effective ways to reach out:

- *Cold-calling:* Classic but powerful—pick up the phone and make a strong first impression.
- *Social media:* Connect where your customers are active. LinkedIn, Instagram, X or Facebook; make them your prospecting playground.
- *Partnerships:* Collaborate with businesses that complement yours; leverage their network to expand your reach.
- *Referrals:* One of the best leads comes through a happy customer's recommendation. Don't be afraid to ask.
- *Email outreach:* Send brief, personalised emails with a clear call to action. Stand out in their inbox by addressing their needs directly.

- *Networking events:* Meet prospects in person at industry events and trade shows. Face-to-face connections leave a lasting impact.
- *Content marketing:* Share valuable insights through blogs, videos or articles. When prospects see your expertise, they'll come to you.

Let me share a few of my favourites in more detail.

Cold-calling: Breaking the Ice Effectively

In sales, a 'cold call' is your first reach-out to a potential customer who doesn't know you yet. The goal is simple: move the sale forward, even if just by a small step. During my years at Maruti Suzuki, I developed a cold-calling approach that transformed team results at dealerships:

- *Research before you call:* Know who you're calling. I made sure the team understood the profile of each B2C prospect by analysing their buying history or publicly available information (in case of B2B opportunities).
- *Have a clear objective:* Each call needs a purpose. When I trained my teams, I insisted they write down their specific goal for each call before dialling.
- *Craft a strong opening statement:* Spark curiosity immediately. For example: 'Hi, this is Rohit from MG Motors. We've just launched a model specifically designed for executives who love to go on off-roading drives. Based on your location, I thought you might be interested in how it could help you in having great adventures—the right way.'

- *Listen and prepare for objections:* In my training workshops, I would always emphasise that listening is more important than talking. Prepare for common objections, but also truly hear what the customer is saying.
- *Keep it natural:* I've recorded thousands of successful calls, and they all have one thing in common—they sound like genuine conversations, not robotic pitches.
- *Focus on benefits, not features:* While training sales teams on selling cars, I inculcated a habit in them of not talking about engine specifications without explaining how those specs translated to a smoother commute or better fuel efficiency.
- *Be patient and persistent:* During market downturns, my most successful team members were those who maintained consistent calling schedules regardless of rejection rates.

Remember: cold calls are just conversations between two people. The moment you see it as anything more intimidating, you've already lost.

Social Media Prospecting: The Digital Gold Mine

Social media is more than just a scrolling distraction; it's a gold mine for reaching new customers. As someone who's built a substantial following on platforms like Instagram and LinkedIn, I can tell you that tapping into this potential means knowing the right platform for your audience.

Here's my personal playbook:

- *LinkedIn, the professional gold mine:* When I was transitioning my career towards leadership consulting, I turned LinkedIn into my primary prospecting tool by:
  - Writing thought leadership articles on industry trends
  - Connecting systematically with decision-makers at target companies
  - Using Sales Navigator to identify and track high-value prospects
  - Participating actively in industry-specific groups.

This approach generated over 40 per cent of my high-value consulting leads within six months, proving far more effective than traditional networking.

- *Instagram, for visual storytelling:* For consumer products, Instagram becomes invaluable. One can make the best use of it by:
  - Posting authentic behind-the-scenes content that humanises your brand
  - Using Instagram stories to create urgency around limited-time offers
  - Leveraging direct messaging for personal, non-scripted conversations
  - Studying analytics religiously to understand what content triggers engagement.

- *WhatsApp, the relationship builder:* WhatsApp might seem casual, but it's become one of my most powerful tools for maintaining relationships. You can use it to:
  - Create segmented broadcast lists for different customer categories
  - Share personalised festival greetings with subtle product mentions
  - Use status updates to showcase customer success stories
  - Respond promptly to inquiries—I aim for under five minutes during business hours.

Of course, there are many more platforms besides the ones I have mentioned—X, Facebook, Pinterest, YouTube, TikTok and other niches. But the key to being successful on any of them is to understand what works on that particular platform.

Remember the young Delhi entrepreneur—the Vada Pav Girl—who turned a simple street food stall into a multi-crore business? Her success wasn't just about the food, it was about the story she shared. Through social media, she consistently posted not only her products but her personal journey: the early struggles, the daily hustle and her dreams. She connected with people by being authentic and relatable. That's not just good content, that's powerful prospecting.

It's the same principle I teach in my workshops today—when you show the real you, you don't just attract customers, you build a community.

One more success story is that of Sridhar Vembu, the CEO of Zoho Corporation, a leading Indian software company offering CRM, email marketing and other business tools. Vembu uses X to engage potential customers, answer questions and share valuable insights on business and tech. His social media presence has helped Zoho attract and convert new customers. For instance, when a small business owner tweeted about an issue with their website, Vembu responded personally, offering advice that ultimately turned the business owner into a Zoho customer.

The Power of Referrals: Your Satisfied Customers as Advocates

Over the years, I've learnt that generating referrals isn't just a sales technique—it's an art form that requires authenticity and perfect timing. When happy clients recommend your products or services, you tap into a trust that's often stronger than any marketing campaign could achieve.

The golden rule that I've discovered after twenty-five years in leadership positions is that the way you ask for referrals matters more than the asking itself. For example, at Maruti Suzuki, we had a system called 'The 3-Day Rule' that tripled our referral rate:

- *Day 1:* Perfect delivery experience
- *Day 2:* Personal follow-up call with genuine curiosity about their experience
- *Day 3:* A specific, confident referral request.

For example, after confirming a customer is delighted with their new vehicle, the executive would say: 'Rajiv-ji, I'm so glad you're enjoying your new Swift. I specifically work with busy professionals like yourself who value efficiency. Would you happen to know one or two colleagues who might appreciate the same experience you've had?'

This specificity transforms vague promises into concrete introductions.

The rewards matter too, but timing is crucial. In my teams, we always reward customers after their referral has converted—never before. This ensures authentic recommendations and creates a moment of unexpected delight when the customer receives their thank-you gift.

I remember when Vikas Prabhu, one of our most satisfied customers, referred three colleagues within a month. Rather than sending the standard gift basket, I suggested a surprise car detailing service at his office, complete with a small celebration. The story spread throughout his company, generating four more leads within weeks.

When asking for referrals, confidence is key. I train my teams to ask with the same assurance they'd use when offering an upgrade: 'Based on your experience, I'd love to help two of your colleagues achieve the same satisfaction. Could you introduce me?'

Partnerships and Collaborations: Strength in Numbers

I have always prioritised what we later called 'Industry-first Partnerships'—strategic alliances that revolutionised our approach to prospecting.

The most successful was what I called the 'Experience Exchange'. We would partner with luxury watch retailers, premium real estate developers and even a chain of five-star hotels. The concept was simple but powerful: create seamless customer experiences across complementary luxury purchases.

For example, when clients bought property in a premium development, they received an exclusive invitation to a private auto showcase event held at the development's clubhouse. This wasn't just a car display; it was a tailored experience where we demonstrated how our vehicles complemented their new lifestyle.

The results were remarkable. These partnerships generated leads with an 80 per cent higher conversion rate than traditional channels, and the average transaction value increased by 22 per cent.

The key insight I've gained from encouraging B2B partnerships is that they must be genuine extensions of your customer's journey, not merely cross-promotion opportunities. I train sales professionals to ask: 'What other significant purchase decisions is my customer making around the same time?' Some powerful combinations I've seen succeed:

- Tractor purchase mela for farmers with cars on display
- An organic grocery chain partnering with fitness studios
- Wedding planners collaborating with honeymoon travel specialists

- Business coaching services aligning with premium co-working spaces
- A real estate agency collaborating with an interior designer
- A pet groomer partnering with a local vet clinic.

The most successful partnerships I've built share three characteristics: complementary (not competitive) offerings, similar customer values and a mutual commitment to exceptional service standards.

Summing Up

When I wrote my bestseller *Fall, Don't Fail*, I discovered that success principles remain consistent across different fields. Vikram, the protagonist in my book, zeroes down to two key success factors: skills and connects. The same is true for prospecting—it's not just the first step in sales, it's the foundation that determines whether you'll build a palace or a sandcastle.

In my role as a laughter yoga facilitator, I often tell newbies that proper breathing is not optional—it's essential for life itself. So is the case with prospecting. Without strategic prospecting, you end up being a farmer waiting for rain instead of one building an irrigation system.

After transforming multiple teams across Birla Cement, General Motors, Maruti Suzuki and Bajaj Auto—as also in the social sector and agri-tech companies—I've distilled my approach into the 'Human-centric Prospecting Framework'—a system that has consistently produced results across industries.

Rohit's Two-Minute Wrap-Up

- *Know your ideal customer:* Use the 4P framework to identify and understand your target market.
- *Diversify your approach:* In today's world, multichannel prospecting isn't just more effective; it's necessary. My most successful teams use a minimum of three complementary channels for each campaign.
- *Build meaningful partnerships:* The strongest business relationships are built on mutual value, not convenience. Identify partners whose customers are on a journey that naturally intersects with yours.
- *Master the art of the referral request:* Timing, specificity and genuine appreciation transform casual customers into passionate advocates. Remember the 3-Day Rule: perfect experience, personal follow-up, precise request.
- *Measure, refine, repeat:* The difference between average and exceptional prospecting is systematic improvement. Track not just quantity but quality of leads from each channel.

Whether you're selling motorcycles like I did at Bajaj, high-end luxury cars like Anand does with BMW or stories like Ashwin does with his books, the principle remains unchanged: find the right people, connect meaningfully and watch your success multiply.

STEP 3: REFINE YOUR PITCH

The worst time to think about what you're going to say is the exact moment you're saying it. That's like trying to assemble a parachute after you've jumped out of the plane. And the truth is that I—Anand Prakash—have been guilty of this approach often.

In our previous chapters, we covered gaining knowledge about the product and finding the right customers. Now we arrive at the heart of the matter: your pitch. The thing that separates the sales tigers from the sales kittens.

Think of it this way: a screenplay is the true hero of any Bollywood film. It shapes the journey, breathes life into characters and crafts those unforgettable moments. Without it, even Amitabh Bachchan would be just a tall man with a great voice saying random things. Well, your sales pitch is that screenplay. It can make you a sales hero, or the forgettable extra who gets edited out of the final cut.

As I often tell my teams at BMW Infinity, a good product speaks for itself, but a great pitch makes it sing. And let's be honest, even Lata Mangeshkar needed good lyrics to create a hit song.

From Knowledge to Connection

So, here's where we stand: you've built your product knowledge using SMART. You've translated it into information the customer cares about using FAB and figured out your customer's triggers with ERF. You've identified potential customers using 4P and started prospecting through various channels. Some people are actually willing to talk further. Now what? Host a party? Send them a fruit basket? Write them poetry?

No—now you pitch. And this is where many salespeople falter faster than a smartphone battery at 1 per cent. They think selling is about pushing features or dropping prices like they're shopping for clothes at Lajpat Nagar.

But that's not it at all.

I learnt this lesson early in my career while selling Maruti Suzuki cars. One afternoon, I watched a veteran salesman, Farrokh, at one of our oldest dealerships outsell everyone despite having the same product knowledge and customer leads. While the rest of us were reciting specifications like we'd memorised a textbook, he was connecting like he'd found his long-lost cousin.

His secret? He approached customers like a superhero would someone in trouble—by understanding their problem first, and then offering the perfect solution. He was less salesman and more problem-solving Iron Man (minus the fancy suit, though his tie was quite impressive).

Customers don't want to be sold to; they want their needs understood and their problems solved. Would you rather listen to a shopkeeper pushing random products or a friend helping you find exactly what you need? Unless that random product happens to be the exact thing you've been searching for across seven cities, I think we both know the answer.

To succeed in sales, you need to be that friend—someone who listens, understands and offers solutions that feel tailored and relevant. Be the person who fixes problems, not the one who creates new ones by talking endlessly about features nobody asked for.

The IDEA Framework for Pitching

After years of training sales teams and watching thousands of pitches, I've developed the IDEA framework for pitches—Identify, Demonstrate, Engage, Apply. It's a step-by-step approach that makes every pitch feel personal.

Identify: Identify the Customer's Needs

The first step is understanding what truly matters to the customer. Instead of jumping straight into your product's features, start by asking questions that encourage them to share their pain points and desires.

When I was selling Honda motorcycles, I never started by talking about engine capacity. Instead, I'd ask, 'What do you use your current bike for?' or 'What frustrates you most about your daily commute?'

These questions help them articulate their wants. If you're selling an instant cookpot, you might ask, 'What dishes are the most time-consuming for you to prepare?' If they say biryani, you could respond with, 'Biryani can feel like a whole-day affair, right? So much prep and timing involved.'

Demonstrate: Highlight the Impact of the Problem

Once you understand the customer's needs, the next step is to empathise and bring out the consequences of not solving the problem. Show that you recognise their frustrations and the impact on their daily life.

Returning to the cookpot example, you may say, 'It's not just the time it takes but the stress of getting it perfect. One small mistake, and it's not biryani—it's pulao.'

I remember a customer at a dealership who mentioned his back pain during long drives. Instead of immediately pointing to the seats' lumbar support, I remember our star salesman saying, 'Back pain can really ruin a drive, can't it? Even the most beautiful route becomes unbearable when you're uncomfortable. And stopping every hour for stretching eats into your travel time.'

This demonstration of understanding deepens the connection and validates their concerns.

Engage: Paint a Picture of Life with Your Product

Now that the problem is clear, engage the customer by helping them visualise how their life improves with your product. Don't just describe benefits; create a mental movie where they're the star, and your product is the trusty sidekick that saves the day.

For the cookpot, you could say, 'Imagine a biryani that's perfectly cooked every single time. No more early mornings prepping or hovering over the stove like you're performing a scientific experiment. Just press a button, go about your day, and come back to a biryani so good your mother-in-law will ask for the recipe—twice.'

When I sold my first BMW 5 Series to a busy executive who complained about his back pain and noisy commute, I didn't just list features like I was reading from a restaurant menu. Instead, I painted a picture:

'Imagine ending your workday and stepping into a cabin that's as quiet as a library—but one where nobody gives you dirty looks for sneezing. Your seat remembers your exact preferences better than your spouse. Your phone connects automatically, traffic updates appear on the screen and that back pain you mentioned is gone, thanks to the dynamic support system that adjusts as you drive. It's like having a personal masseuse built into your car, minus the awkward small talk.'

His eyes lit up like Diwali had come early, and I knew he was mentally already driving the car home.

Apply: Offer a Customised Product Solution

Now it's time to introduce your product as the perfect solution. Focus on how specific features solve their specific problems.

For the cookpot, you could say, 'Our instant cookpot has a flavour-lock feature and anti-burn technology, so your biryani comes out perfect every time. With this, you can relax and entertain guests instead of stressing in the kitchen.'

With my BMW customer, I concluded with: 'The 5 Series has an advanced driver's seat with sixteen-way adjustment, including lumbar support that dynamically changes during your drive. The cabin is insulated with acoustic glass that keeps out 90 per cent of road noise, and the suspension reads the road ahead to smooth out bumps before you even feel them.'

IDEA in Action: More Examples

Let me show you how this framework applies across different products:

For a luxury mattress to a health-conscious customer:

- *Identify:* 'How does your current mattress affect your sleep quality?'
- *Demonstrate:* 'A mattress that doesn't support well can really impact your energy and focus the next day.'
- *Engage:* 'Imagine waking up feeling completely refreshed, without any back pain or stiffness.'
- *Apply:* 'Our mattress has memory foam that aligns to your body, providing support and comfort for an uninterrupted, restful night.'

For noise-cancelling headphones to a traveller:

- *Identify:* 'What's the hardest part of long flights for you?'

- *Demonstrate:* 'It's exhausting trying to sleep with all the background noise, right?'
- *Engage:* 'Imagine a flight where you slip on your headphones, block out all distractions and arrive at your destination feeling rested.'
- *Apply:* 'These headphones offer top-of-the-line noise cancellation and twenty-hour battery life, which is perfect for travel. Just peace, quiet and comfort on every trip.'

For an insurance plan for a young family:

- *Identify:* 'What's most important when you think about your family's future?'
- *Demonstrate:* 'Planning for the future is tough with so many unknowns, especially with young kids.'
- *Engage:* 'Imagine knowing your family's future is secure, no matter what. Peace of mind for you and a safety net for them.'
- *Apply:* 'This plan covers both life and health insurance, providing comprehensive protection and savings, tailored to give your family security as they grow.'

Active Listening: Two Ears, One Closed Mouth

There's a joke among the sales teams I have trained: the best sales pitch starts with two ears and one closed mouth. If God wanted us to talk more than listen, he'd have given us two mouths and one ear. By following this rule, you'll find that selling becomes less about persuasion and more about genuinely helping.

Active listening is less hearing and more understanding. It's the difference between a doctor who nods and thinks about lunch as you talk about your painful knee, and one who actually figures out why your knee makes that weird clicking sound when you dance to Bollywood songs.

I train my team to paraphrase what the customer says, affirm their concerns and align our solutions to their needs. Customers want to feel valued, not sold to. They want to feel understood, and not to be thought of as ATMs with legs.

Use SPIN to Listen

To structure your listening, I recommend the SPIN technique developed by author and consultant Neil Rackham: Situation, Problem, Implication, Need-Payoff.

S	*Situation*	Understand the customer's current situation
P	*Problem*	Reveal customer pain points
I	*Implication*	Create urgency for change
N	*Need-Payoff*	Lead buyers to conclude on their own

Situation Questions

These gather background information about the customer's current situation.

- 'What car are you driving right now?'
- 'How long have you had it?'
- 'What do you use it most often for?'

Problem Questions

These uncover issues or challenges the prospect is facing.

- 'What aspects of your current car are frustrating?'
- 'Do you ever wish it had more space/power/features?'
- 'How does it handle your daily commute?'

Implication Questions

These emphasise the consequences of the problems uncovered.

- 'How does that lack of space affect your family trips?'
- 'What happens when you need to drive clients around in your current car?'
- 'How much extra time does slow acceleration cost you in traffic?'

Need-Payoff Questions

These focus on the benefits of solving the identified issues.

- 'Would more cargo space make weekend trips easier?'
- 'How valuable would it be to have a car that projects professionalism to your clients?'
- 'If you could cut fifteen minutes off your commute with better performance, how would that benefit your day?'

I've found SPIN particularly useful in complex sales, where understanding the buyer's deeper needs is essential for building trust.

Varying the Pitch According to Customers

There's a saying in Hindi: *paanchon ungliyan ek sammaan nahin hoti hain.* None of the five fingers is alike. Think of it like trying to feed the same food to your entire family, but your father wants it spicy, your mother wants it less oily, your brother wants extra ghee and your health-conscious sister wants to know if you used olive oil. It reminds me that every customer is unique, even when they're shopping for the same product.

Here's a success story. Nisreen, a colleague who used to be part of a Honda dealership, now works at a Samsung store in Srinagar, having moved back from Delhi. She handles customers with a wide range of needs. She told me about a sales target that she needed to hit for Samsung Fold models—and then three customers walked into her store.

For a housewife with simple needs, Nisreen highlighted the stunning picture quality, camera features and smooth access to social media apps. For a working professional, she emphasised long battery life, ample storage and compatibility with Galaxy Buds and fitness watches. For a style-savvy Gen Z customer, she showcased the Fold's bold colour options, sleek swivel modes and enhanced video features perfect for creating eye-catching reels.

The key isn't just listening; it's tuning in to what's unsaid. It's about observing, understanding and responding with precision. Often, customers don't even realise what they need until you reveal it to them.

Here's how a salesman may vary his pitch when selling water purifiers in Delhi:

Audience Type	Key Concerns	Pitch Focus	Pitch Customisation
Urban Professionals	Health, convenience	Cutting-edge technology, advanced filtration	Include brand preferences, customer service provisions
Rural Households	Affordability, reliability	Cost-effective, durable, water storage options	Use local language, increase trust, rural EMI schemes
Small Businesses	Efficiency	Long-term savings, reliability	ROI, scalability
Elderly	Health, simplicity	Benefits, simple operation	Ease of use, safety, installation, demo, maintenance services

Creating a Concise and Compelling Pitch

When we watch a movie, what touches our hearts the most? The brilliant dialogues that make us believe in the characters and relate to them. Similarly, in sales, the only way to connect to customers' beliefs is to deliver a concise and compelling pitch.

Many salespeople make a common mistake. They think that delivering a long monologue filled with technical terms can impress customers. That's absolutely false. Customers simply don't have all day available until you reach the crux.

Here's my simple guide to developing your pitch:

- *Grab attention:* Start strong with a catchy statement, question or bold fact. This should immediately pull the customer into the conversation.
- *Build a connection:* Tell a brief story or share a relatable experience. Make the product feel personal to the customer's world.
- *Highlight the relevance:* Show exactly how the product fits into the customer's life, addressing their needs and concerns.
- *Keep it direct:* Use simple, clear language, focusing only on essential points. Don't overload with details—just what matters most.
- *Speak conversationally:* Use natural, friendly language that feels like a conversation, not a lecture.
- *Reinforce the benefits:* Emphasise the main benefits in a way that highlights why they matter to the customer right now.

A pitch must be memorable. This is why jingles like *'Fevicol ka jod hai, tootega nahi'* and Asian Paints' *'Har ghar kuch kehta hai'* work so well. That power of touching hearts and creating an instant mark on the customer is the magic X-factor that helps you sell the product.

With this guideline, I keep my pitches between 30 and 120 seconds long depending on the circumstances, focusing on covering all the content under IDEA.

Practice Makes Perfect

In perhaps every language, the importance of abhyas, or dedicated practice, has been highlighted. My father taught me, 'Practice makes a man perfect, but only if he's practising the right thing. Otherwise, he just becomes perfectly wrong.'

A perfect pitch cannot be created out of thin air, just like a perfect roti doesn't magically appear the first time you slap dough between your palms. For this, you need lots of practice, and the process takes some time as it involves correcting your inherent approaches.

When I first started selling cars, I would record myself on my phone, then listen to it during my commute. It was more painful than sitting through a five-hour family function where your relatives keep asking why you're not married yet. I rambled, repeated myself and used so many filler words that 'umm' and 'you know' could have sponsored my career. But after weeks of practice, I developed a natural, confident delivery that didn't sound rehearsed. I went from sounding like a nervous teenager asking someone on a date to someone who knew what he was talking about.

Using testimonials, case studies and success stories as proof of your product's value is a smart move. I often share stories like, 'One of our clients improved their daily commute by 40 per cent after switching to this model.' But I practise these in advance so they flow naturally, not like I'm reading my daughter's school essay at gunpoint.

I also use the technique of introducing higher price points first to make standard offers feel more reasonable. For instance, I present our premium package before our basic option.

As Omar Periu, the peak performance coach, says, 'Sales success comes after you stretch yourself past your limits on a daily basis.' So, are you ready to begin your pitching practice sessions? Here's my practical guide:

Technique	What it involves	Benefit	Additional tips
Mirror practice	Practise in front of a mirror	Improves facial expressions	Focus on maintaining eye contact
Peer feedback	Get feedback from colleagues	Identifies areas of improvement	Take notes during feedback
Role-playing	Simulate different customer scenarios	Prepares you for various objections	Focus on realistic objections
Recording	Record and review your pitch	Allows self-evaluation	Pay attention to tone and pace
Script rehearsal	Memorise key parts of your pitch	Ensures consistency	Emphasise main selling points
Mock presentations	Present to a small group	Builds confidence	Ask for honest feedback

Technique	What it involves	Benefit	Additional tips
Time-limited practice	Practise delivering the pitch within a set time	Enhances time management skills	Stay concise and focused
Objection handling	Practise responding to common objections	Improves response skills	Use real objections for practice
Audience engagement	Practise engaging with the audience	Boosts interaction skills	Ask questions to involve audience
Emotional appeal	Focus on connecting emotionally with the audience	Strengthens emotional connections	Use relatable anecdotes
Tech utilisation (optional)	Incorporate technology in practice	Enhances tech presentation skills	Practise with different tools

Your pitches should feel genuine, not forced. Building an emotional connection is crucial. Some salespeople sound robotic because they're too focused on delivering a rehearsed pitch word-for-word. If they forget a line or get distracted, they start fumbling, leaving a poor impression.

Facts tell, but stories sell. I share relatable anecdotes that evoke emotions, helping customers visualise my product as part of their lives. Emotional resonance creates loyalty.

Be ready for any scenario—a customer asking for more details, or someone in a rush needing your pitch in a sentence or two. Have pitches tailored to every timeframe.

Case Study: Farhaan's Step-By-Step Pitch Strategy

Let me share a success story from my network. Farhaan works at HelloPay Credit Systems, selling credit cards in Chennai. Targeting young professionals, he's crafted a pitch designed to address their key needs: flexibility, value and savings.

- *He first understands the customer profile.* Farhaan's target audience is young professionals in Chennai. They are value conscious and look for cards that cater to diverse spending habits without sacrificing savings.
- *He starts with a storytelling hook.* Farhaan opens with a question that hooks attention. 'What if you had a credit card that gave you 3X reward points on shopping, exclusive global offers and zero annual fees? Imagine going to the movies every month, courtesy of cashbacks.'
- *Next, he highlights key benefits.* 'The product has no hidden fees or annual charges, and you can redeem points at the store or for mobile recharges. Plus, as a new cardholder, you get complimentary airport lounge access—four times a year for domestic and twice for international travel. And that's not all. You'll enjoy a 1.5 per cent discount on fuel top-ups, helping you save on everyday expenses.'

- *He makes it relatable.* Farhaan aligns the card's features with his customer's lifestyle: 'For busy professionals like you, the card is easy to use domestically and internationally, online or offline. Repayment is flexible, with convenient EMI options. If one month's budget is tight, simply convert your purchases to no-cost EMIs with one click! And paying is hassle-free—you can use CRED, UPI, Amazon Pay, net-banking and more.'
- *He perfects his pitch.* Farhaan practises with hand gestures and a conversational style, ensuring he's comfortable and ready to deliver it naturally, adapting for each customer.
- *He prepares for objections.* If a customer hesitates, Farhaan responds by reinforcing the card's value: 'It's normal to be cautious. But right now, you're getting a lifetime free credit card plus inaugural vouchers from top brands. Think of it as a smart investment—a payment tool that's flexible, worry free and lets you manage your finances your way. With us, you control the dates, payments and budget. There's no better time to unlock these benefits.'

A pitch is a powerful tool that can close a sale on the spot—if crafted well. It's like having a superpower. I've seen this countless times across my career from selling nuts and bolts (literally, not figuratively) to luxury vehicles that cost more than some people's houses. Developing a perfect pitch takes hard work, continuous improvement and plenty of practice. It's not like instant noodles but more like a slow-cooked dal makhani—it takes time and effort to get it just right.

Start by capturing the customer's attention from the very first moment. Use a catchy hook—an intriguing fact, a thought-provoking question or a relatable scenario—to make a strong first impression because you never get a second chance to make a first impression!

Anand's Rundown

- *IDEA framework:* Use the IDEA framework—Identify, Demonstrate, Engage, Apply—to shape a pitch that feels tailored, empathetic and helpful.
- *Customer as the hero:* Make the customer feel like the central figure in the story. Show them how the product can directly address their challenges, improve their life or make their work easier.
- *Adaptability in pitching:* A one-size-fits-all approach won't be as effective. Customise the pitch based on the customer's profile, needs and preferences.
- *Conciseness and clarity:* An impactful pitch is clear, to the point and free from excessive jargon. Using everyday language that speaks directly to the customer's needs keeps them engaged and builds trust.
- *Emotional connection:* Use relatable examples and positive body language to create an authentic connection, making the pitch feel more like a conversation than a sales tactic.
- *Handling objections with empathy:* Be prepared to address customer hesitations by reinforcing the

product's value in a way that feels supportive and aligned with their concerns.
- *Practice makes perfect:* Use techniques like mirror practice, peer feedback, role-playing and timed practice to refine your delivery, build confidence and ensure you are ready for different scenarios.
- *Trust and authenticity:* A well-delivered pitch is about more than just selling; it's about helping customers feel heard and understood, building trust and positioning yourself as a problem-solver rather than just a salesperson.

STEP 4: OPTIMISE THE FUNNEL

Ever wonder why some salespeople close deals while the rest of the team struggles? I'll tell you their secret: they've mastered the art of the sales funnel.

See, the superstar salespeople I've worked with don't just 'sell'. They carefully guide prospects from that first curious glance all the way to the triumphant handshake of a deal closed. They anticipate every step, answer every question before it's asked and gently nudge leads down the funnel until 'maybe' transforms into 'absolutely'.

Yours truly, Anand Prakash, had to learn this through many knocks. In my early days selling Honda bikes, I'd excitedly pitch features to anyone I met and then wonder why they weren't pulling out their wallets on the spot. I was trying to jump straight from 'hello' to 'here's your receipt'—skipping all the crucial stages in between.

The sales funnel isn't just a fancy marketing term; it's a complete sales system. Think of it as planning a journey with your prospective client where you've already mapped out all the scenic viewpoints and rest stops, eliminating any chance they'll take a wrong turn. When you manage your funnel properly, you're not just closing more deals; you're building relationships that generate referrals and repeat business for years to come.

Let me walk you through how to make your sales funnel absolutely unstoppable.

The Five Stages Every Sale Must Pass Through

When I train my sales teams, I emphasise that every purchase—whether it's a ₹5-lakh car or a ₹50-crore luxury home—passes through five essential stages: Awareness, Interest, Intent, Decision and Loyalty. Skip one, and you'll watch your prospect walking away.

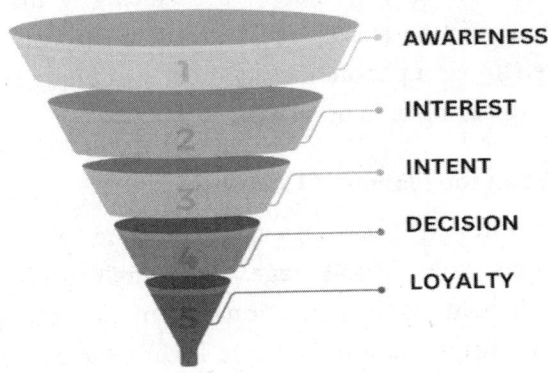

Awareness: Get on Their Radar

As Chris Grosser, the motivational speaker, rightly said, 'Opportunities don't happen. You create them.'

You need to be creating visibility, or top-of-mind awareness (TOMA). Think of it as casting a wide net to capture attention. Whether it's through an eye-catching ad, a compelling social media post or a well-timed email, your job here is to make prospects aware of your solution. A friendly conversation starter: 'Have you seen our latest offer?' This question could kick off a conversation, piquing interest in your product.

When we were launching the BMW X7 in Delhi, instead of just another boring print ad, we partnered with upscale malls to display the vehicle in high-traffic areas where our target customers shopped. We also placed targeted ads on social media feeds of users who matched our ideal customer profile.

You're not selling yet, merely introducing yourself. A simple conversation starter like, 'Have you seen our latest X7 model? It has a panoramic sky roof!' can pique interest without pressuring for a purchase.

Interest: Fan the Flames of Curiosity

Now that you've got their attention, it's time to fan those flames of curiosity. At this stage, I train my team to share valuable insights and educational content that keeps prospects engaged. Some fantastic luxury car companies (including Mercedes-Benz) have done this by creating short video demonstrations of the unique features, particularly an FAQ section addressing common concerns about electric vehicles.

Let's say you're selling fitness equipment. A blog post about creating an effective home gym set-up could engage prospects who are still exploring their options.

At the interest stage, give freely without expecting an immediate return. It's like dating—you don't propose on the first date, do you (unless you're in a particularly dramatic Bollywood movie)?

Intent: Reading the Buying Signals

This is where the magic starts happening. The buyer is now seriously considering making a purchase, and your job is to make that decision feel both logical and emotionally satisfying.

In my organisation, we recognise intent when customers start asking specific questions about financing options, delivery timelines or comparing similar models. These are buying signals—clear indicators they're mentally preparing to own the product.

When I notice a customer reaching this stage, I might offer something exclusive: 'Since you're considering the 5 Series, we have a limited-time offer that includes complimentary accessories worth ₹50,000 if you book this week.' A time-bound incentive creates a gentle urgency without feeling pushy.

The key is to pick up on verbal cues and body language. If they're leaning in, asking detailed questions or requesting a second test drive with their spouse, they're showing intent. Personalise your pitch and present a compelling reason to act soon.

Think about your own recent purchases. What pushed you over the edge? Was it a discount? A trial period? A perfectly timed email addressing that one concern you had? Use those insights to craft your intent-stage offers.

Decision: Make Buying Ridiculously Easy

Your prospect is ready to buy, so don't fumble the ball on the goal line!

I've seen too many dealings lost at this critical stage because of complicated paperwork, unclear next steps or simply poor communication. In my organisation, we've streamlined our purchase process to make it almost effortless. We offer doorstep delivery of documents, digital signatures for most paperwork and multiple payment options.

I always tell my team: 'At the decision stage, your job is to remove every possible obstacle between the customer and ownership.'

To a customer who's ready to proceed, we might say: 'We offer both online and offline payment options, as well as customised financing plans with EMIs that suit your budget. Which would work best for you?' Notice that we're not asking *if* they want to buy, but *how* they prefer to complete the purchase.

Loyalty: The Sale Is Just the Beginning

Congratulations, the sale is closed, but your work isn't over. Nurturing loyalty involves more than a thank-you email. If you think your job ends when the customer puts down the deposit on her new flat, you're missing out on the most profitable stage of the funnel.

I learnt early in my career that nurturing loyalty costs far less than acquiring new customers. Some of the best companies have built a comprehensive post-purchase engagement strategy that turns buyers into brand ambassadors.

After delivery, each customer receives a personal thank-you message from me, followed by an invitation to exclusive owner events. We send anniversary cards on the purchase date, offer special service packages and maintain regular contact through our newsletter.

Think about your own best post-purchase experiences. What made you feel valued as a customer? Was it the follow-up, the special offers or just feeling like you weren't forgotten after your money changed hands? Use those insights to build loyalty programmes that keep customers coming back.

The Café Conundrum: How I Became a Regular

Let me give you a simple example that shows how effective funnels work in everyday life.

A few years back, I was walking near Khan Market on a particularly chilly Delhi morning when the aroma of freshly ground coffee wafted from a new café I'd barely noticed before. What caught my eye wasn't just the smell but a chalkboard sign that read: 'Free Sample of Our House Special Caramel Latte—Come, Warm Up!'

My curiosity piqued (that's *awareness*), I stepped inside. The barista handed me a small cup saying, 'Let me know what you think, sir. We roast the beans ourselves!' The drink was rich, perfectly balanced between bitter and sweet. Soon, I was asking about their coffee sources and noticing the cosy atmosphere with power outlets at every table—perfect for working remotely (that's *interest*).

As I savoured the sample, the barista casually mentioned, 'By the way, we have a loyalty programme. Buy nine drinks and get the tenth free. Plus, if you sign up today, your first full cup is half-price' (that's *intent*). Well, my office was nearby, and I did need a good coffee spot for client meetings, so I found myself joining their programme and promising to return.

The following week, I came back, and, remarkably, the barista remembered my name. 'The usual caramel latte, Mr Prakash?' The purchase process was smooth—they even had a contactless payment option. Within minutes, I was sipping my coffee and setting up my laptop (that's *decision*).

Over the next month, they kept me engaged. I received an email about their new pastry selection from a local bakery, an invitation to a weekend 'Coffee Appreciation' workshop and occasional messages with special offers (that's *loyalty*). Soon enough, I was not just a customer but an advocate, bringing colleagues there for meetings and recommending it to friends.

See how seamlessly they moved me through every stage of the funnel? I went from a random passer-by to a regular customer who brought them more business—all because they had a system in place to guide me from awareness to loyalty.

Real-World Funnel Success Stories

Let me share two success stories from sales professionals I know who've mastered funnel management.

Amit's Story

Amit is an insurance adviser at ICICI Lombard, Mumbai. His company partners with American Express to give him exclusive leads, but it's his funnel strategy that converts them at nearly double the industry average.

For *awareness*, Amit sends personalised WhatsApp messages introducing himself and the special insurance rates available only to Amex customers. There's no hard sell—just a friendly heads-up about the exclusive offer.

When prospects show *interest*, he offers free fifteen-minute consultations over WhatsApp, shares relatable client stories and sends simplified explainers about term insurance and unit linked insurance plans. One clever touch: he creates short videos answering the top questions he receives.

For customers showing *intent* by requesting quotes, Amit customises options to fit their specific budget and family needs. He addresses concerns proactively and highlights time-limited promotional offers to create gentle urgency.

At the *decision* stage, Amit makes the application process ridiculously simple with a mobile-friendly system. He guides customers through each step personally, making a possibly complex process feel effortless.

To build *loyalty*, he conducts annual WhatsApp check-ins to update coverage as life changes occur. He's also created a referral programme that rewards existing clients for introductions. Most brilliantly, he sends timely reminders about tax benefits from their policies before the financial year ends—something his clients particularly appreciate.

Priya's Story

Priya, meanwhile, is a wellness consultant at NM Medical Centre, Pune. Her funnel strategy addresses the specific health concerns and time limitations of busy corporate executives.

For *awareness*, she partners with corporate offices to distribute educational materials about executive health risks and preventive care. Her targeted LinkedIn posts speak directly to the concerns of high-stress professionals.

When executives show *interest*, Priya sends a follow-up WhatsApp message with a free 'Health Tips for Executives' e-book. She also organises thirty-minute lunch-and-learn sessions at corporate offices, making preventive healthcare feel accessible and relevant.

For clients who show *intent* by booking an initial consultation, she offers personalised health packages based on age, stress levels and specific health concerns. She's particularly effective at addressing scheduling concerns by offering early morning and weekend appointment slots.

At the *decision* stage, Priya ensures a seamless booking experience with minimal paperwork and flexible appointment times. She's persuaded the medical centre to implement a dedicated fast-track check-in for corporate clients.

To build *loyalty*, Priya follows each check-up with a personalised health report and wellness plan delivered via WhatsApp. She schedules annual reminders for regular check-ups, and has created a corporate referral programme where clients earn discounts by recommending colleagues.

My Secret Strategies for Effective Funnel Management

After years of refining sales funnels across multiple businesses, I've identified five strategies that consistently deliver results, regardless of what you're selling.

1. Define Crystal-Clear Goals for Each Funnel Stage

You wouldn't start a road trip without knowing your destination, right? Each stage of your funnel needs specific, measurable objectives.

At a friend's real estate company, they set precise targets: their awareness campaigns must reach 1 lakh qualified prospects monthly, their interest content should generate 2,000 information requests, their intent stage must produce 200 site visits, the decision process should convert 40 per cent of site visits and their loyalty programme should generate 25 per cent of new leads through referrals.

Write these goals down, and ensure every action aligns with them. For example: 'During the awareness stage, my goal is to increase website visitors by 25 per cent through targeted social media campaigns.'

2. Master the Art of Lead Scoring

Not all leads are equal, and your time is precious. I learnt this lesson by chasing every lead with equal vigour—and watching my conversion rates suffer.

Now, I use a simple scoring system that assigns points based on prospect behaviour. For example:

- Visited pricing page: 10 points
- Downloaded brochure: 15 points
- Attended webinar: 20 points
- Requested a call back: 30 points
- Booked a test drive or site visit: 50 points

Leads with higher scores get priority attention. Even without fancy CRM software, you can create a basic Excel spreadsheet to track and score leads. The key is consistency—update your scores with every interaction.

3. Personalise Every Interaction

Mass messages get mass-ignored. I've seen conversion rates triple when my team switches from generic communications to personalised outreach.

For example, if a prospect has been browsing our X5 SUV models online, our follow-up doesn't just say, 'Thanks for visiting BMW Infinity.' Instead, it says, 'I noticed you've been exploring our X5 models. As someone who appreciates powerful SUVs, you might be interested in these three features that make the X5 stand out ...'

Every detail you remember and reference shows the customer they're valued. As American businessman W. Clement Stone aptly put it, 'Sales are contingent upon the attitude of the salesman—not the attitude of the prospect.'

4. Deliver the Right Content at the Right Time

Content is king, but context is queen—and she runs the household. At each funnel stage, customers need different information:
- During *awareness*, they need attention-grabbing content that introduces your solution—think social media posts, blogs and ads.
- During *interest*, they need educational content that builds understanding—webinars, how-to guides and FAQs.
- During *intent*, they need content that confirms they're making the right choice—comparisons, reviews and case studies.
- During *decision*, they need information that makes buying easy—straightforward pricing, clear next steps and purchase guides.
- During *loyalty*, they need content that makes them feel valued—exclusive updates, community content and special offers.

We once created a specialised brochure for a model series that only highlighted the entertainment systems because we learnt that a key decision-maker was particularly interested in that aspect. Tailor your content to address the specific questions at each stage of the journey.

5. Use Psychology-Based Triggers to Optimise Conversion

Understanding basic human psychology can transform your funnel efficiency.

For example, electronics retailers often use the principle of scarcity through time-bound offers: 'Only three units of this model variant remain in this configuration.' This creates urgency without being pushy.

Hospitality companies leverage social proof by displaying testimonials from similar customers: 'Here's what other guests say about their stay ...'

When properly applied, these psychological triggers can significantly increase conversion rates at every funnel stage.

Some Key Learnings

Even the best-designed funnel can leak leads if you make these common mistakes. And I've made all of them so that you don't have to.

Don't Neglect Lead Nurturing

Early in my career, I believed that interested leads would naturally progress towards purchase without much hand-holding. I was dead wrong.

Leads cool faster than a cup of chai in Shimla winter. A prospect who was excited about your product on Monday might completely forget about you by Wednesday if you don't maintain contact.

The solution? Scheduled follow-ups with genuine value. Don't just ask, 'Are you ready to buy yet?' Instead, share something interesting: 'I came across this article about XYZ that reminded me of our conversation—thought you might find it useful.'

Avoid Inconsistent Follow-Ups

I once had a promising lead that I followed up intensely for a week, then completely forgot about when a shiny new prospect appeared. Three months later, I discovered he had purchased from a competitor—just one week after my follow-ups stopped.

Now, we have a strict schedule: initial leads receive follow-ups at two days, one week, two weeks, one month and quarterly thereafter—until they either convert or explicitly opt out. This systemised approach ensures no prospect falls through the cracks.

Sales isn't about pressure; it's about trust. Consistency builds that trust brick by brick.

But remember: persistence without respect is just harassment. A prospect once told me, 'I decided to buy from you because you stayed in touch without being annoying.' That's the perfect balance.

Always Re-target Interested Leads

Some leads show clear interest but don't convert immediately. In my early days, I would simply let them go if they didn't purchase after a few conversations.

Now, we have specific re-engagement campaigns. For example, if someone test-drove a car but didn't purchase it, we reach out thirty days later with a different angle—perhaps a special financing option or an invitation to an exclusive event where they can experience the car again.

Email re-targeting and social media remarketing have been particularly effective here.

Our digital marketing team has created sophisticated re-targeting campaigns that show previous visitors ads specifically related to the models they viewed. These ads offer new information or special incentives to bring them back.

Don't Ignore Retention

The biggest mistake I see sales teams make is celebrating when the contract is signed—and then forgetting the customer exists until it's time for renewal or a potential upgrade.

I've now made post-purchase engagement a priority. From personalised delivery experiences to exclusive owner events and dedicated service liaisons, we ensure customers feel valued long after the initial sale.

Remember: satisfied customers don't just return; they refer others. The loyalty stage of your funnel should feed directly back into the awareness stage through referrals and testimonials.

Personalise Every Touchpoint

Generic messages get generic results. I once had a customer tell me he chose my establishment over the competition specifically because 'you remembered I needed extra headroom for my tall family members'.

Make every interaction count. Acknowledge special occasions like birthdays with tailored offers. Reference previous conversations to show you're paying attention. Even small touches—like mentioning the prospect's favourite cricket team after noticing memorabilia during a house visit—can create powerful connections.

Use Technology to Anticipate Needs

Our CRM system flags when a customer's warranty is approaching expiration or when their typical service interval is nearing. This allows us to reach out proactively rather than reactively.

Even without sophisticated technology, you can create simple reminder systems. A basic Excel sheet with purchase dates and follow-up intervals can work wonders.

Make Processes Crystal Clear

Confusion kills conversion. Every communication should include a clear, direct call to action: 'Book your test drive by clicking here' works better than 'Ask for a free test drive'. Why make the customer ask? And no one ever charges for a test drive? So why play up the word 'free'?

On our website, we reduced the steps to book a test drive from five clicks to two—and saw a 20 per cent increase in bookings overnight. The easier you make it to say yes, the more yeses you'll hear.

In my previous job, I mystery-shopped the dealerships and discovered that our financing application required information that many customers didn't have readily available. No wonder our financing conversion was lower than expected.

We simplified the process, allowing customers to complete 90 per cent of the paperwork with just basic information, and saw our financing approval rates jump.

Look critically at every step in your purchase process. Is your website mobile-friendly? Is your payment system simple? Can customers easily reach you with questions? Every obstacle you remove increases your conversion rate.

Leverage Social Proof Strategically

Humans are social creatures—we trust recommendations from others, especially those similar to us. We display testimonials from specific customer segments (business owners, doctors, tech professionals) to build credibility with similar prospects.

One particularly effective tactic was when we created short video testimonials from customers explaining why they chose our product. These videos, featuring people from different professions and life stages, resonate deeply with prospects facing similar decisions.

Offer Real-Time Support

Questions often arise at odd hours when people are browsing online. In my real estate company where we develop and sell residential plots, we implemented a WhatsApp Business account that connects prospects to a sales team member until 10 p.m. daily.

The ability to get immediate answers often prevents prospects from moving on to competitor websites. As one customer put it, 'I messaged three companies with questions at 9 p.m. Only one responded within minutes—that's when I decided who deserved my business.'

My Final Thoughts

Like a trusted tour guide, a well-designed sales funnel leads customers to the best view—the one where they clearly see why they need your product in their lives. I've seen average salespeople become superstars simply by mastering funnel management.

Remember: every 'no' in your funnel isn't a rejection; it's just a 'not yet'. Keep nurturing, adding value and moving prospects toward the next stage. Successful salespeople don't try to close every prospect immediately; they focus on maintaining momentum through the funnel.

A well-managed funnel works like a semi-automated system, continuously generating sales and building customer relationships. It only requires your attentive action, a bit of persuasive magic and a genuine desire to serve your customers' needs.

The best part of mastering your sales funnel? Even leads that don't convert immediately remain in your ecosystem for future opportunities. And those who do convert often become your most powerful marketing channel through word-of-mouth referrals.

Last Words from Anand

- *Nurture leads consistently:* Engage customers at every stage to build trust and maintain momentum through the funnel. Never let a good lead cool off.
- *Attract with value, retain with care:* Use compelling content to spark interest and personalised follow-ups to keep it alive. Always move prospects one step closer to purchase.
- *Re-target with precision:* When leads show interest but don't convert, go back with tailored offers that align with their specific interests. It's often the third or fourth touchpoint that triggers a sale.
- *Make buying ridiculously easy:* Remove every obstacle from the purchase process. The smoother the path to purchase, the higher your conversion rate.
- *Turn customers into advocates:* Transform one-time buyers into lifetime value by creating loyalty programmes that recognise, reward and engage. Your best salespeople are often your existing customers.

STEP 5: MANAGE YOUR TIME

Ancient strategist Chanakya once wrote, 'Even a minute of one's life cannot be obtained—even for a million gold coins.' Dramatic? Perhaps. But as someone who once tried to cram thirty hours of work into a day (spoiler alert: it didn't end well), I—Rohit Goel—can confirm the man was onto something.

Time is a great equaliser. Whether you're a struggling sales rookie or the CEO of a Fortune 500 company, you get exactly twenty-four hours each day. The difference between closing that game-changing deal or watching it slip through your fingers often comes down to how you manage those precious hours.

If I asked you to name a salesperson's most valuable resource, would 'time' make your list? Probably not. Most people say 'relationships' or 'product knowledge'. But after spending twenty-five years in leadership roles in large companies, I know that time management is the secret weapon that separates sales superstars from the eternally struggling.

Prioritise Like Eisenhower

'What's most important today?' We've all asked this question first thing in the morning (usually while desperately chugging coffee). In this field, getting that answer right can make or break your month.

My go-to framework is the Eisenhower Matrix—named after US President Dwight Eisenhower who famously said, 'What is important is seldom urgent, and what is urgent is seldom important.' Here's how I apply it to sales:

	Urgent	Not Urgent
Important	**1. Do It** Examples: client calls, product demos, marketing presentations	**2. Schedule It** Examples: prospecting, follow-ups, updating database
Not Important	**3. Automate It** Examples: uploading blogs social media posts friendly emails to customers	**4. Delete It** Examples: friends' WhatsApp group, random YouTube browsing

Quadrant 1: Important and Urgent (Do First)

This is your VIP quadrant—client meetings, sales pitches, addressing customer complaints and deadline-driven presentations. These tasks directly impact your revenue and require immediate attention. Handle these first, without exceptions.

Quadrant 2: Important but Not Urgent (Schedule)

This is your career-growth quadrant—prospecting, building relationships, personal development and training. These activities don't scream for attention but do determine your long-term success. Block time for these or watch your client pipeline slowly dry up.

Quadrant 3: Urgent but Not Important (Delegate or Automate)

These are the distractions masquerading as priorities—unnecessary meetings, certain administrative tasks and low-value requests from others. Delegate or automate these whenever possible.

Quadrant 4: Neither Important nor Urgent (Eliminate)

These are time-wasters—mindless social media, office gossip, excessive email checking. Be ruthless about eliminating them from your workday.

During my time at Bajaj Auto, I coached a struggling sales representative who swore he was working twelve-hour days but couldn't hit targets. When we tracked his time, the shocking truth emerged: he spent nearly 40 per cent of his day on Quadrant 4 activities! Three months after reorganising his priorities, he was outperforming veterans on the team.

Golden Hours: Timing Is Everything

As a salesperson, *when* you reach out matters as much as *what* you say. I call the peak responsiveness windows 'golden hours'—those magical times when prospects are most likely to engage.

I discovered this by accident during my first year at General Motors. After tracking hundreds of calls, I noticed that conversion rates doubled between 10:30 a.m. and noon compared to late afternoon attempts. This wasn't random luck; it was a pattern I could leverage.

Let me introduce you to Neha, a Mumbai-based insurance agent who transformed her results with this approach. She experimented and discovered her prospects were most responsive between 10 a.m. and noon and again around 4 to 5 p.m. By dedicating these windows exclusively to outreach, she increased her contact rate by 35 per cent and doubled her appointments.

To identify your golden hours:

- *Track response patterns* by time of day for two weeks.
- *Test different communication channels* (some prefer calls in the morning but respond to emails in the evening).
- *Pre-schedule outreach* during peak times, even when you're busy with other tasks.

Once you know when your prospects are most likely to engage, you're not just working hard; you're working smart.

Time Blocking: Structure Creates Freedom

'But, Rohit,' you might say, 'I'm too busy putting out fires to structure my day!' That's exactly why you need time blocking—to escape the endless cycle of reactivity.

Let me share Rajesh's schedule. He is a computer hardware salesman who consistently hits 130 per cent of his targets:

- 8–9.30 a.m.: Prospecting (researching leads, preparing outreach)
- 9.30–11 a.m.: Active outreach (calls, emails during golden hours)
- 11 a.m.–12.30 p.m.: Client meetings/demos
- 12.30–1 p.m.: Quick lunch
- 1–2.30 p.m.: Follow-ups (nurturing existing leads)
- 2.30–4 p.m.: Admin work (CRM updates, reports)
- 4–5.30 p.m.: Learning (product training, skill development)
- 5.30–6.30 p.m.: Second outreach window
- 6.30–7 p.m.: Review and planning (tomorrow's priorities)

The beauty of this approach isn't just organisation, it's psychological. Each block allows you to do focused work, eliminating the mental fatigue of constantly switching between tasks. When Rajesh calls prospects, he does not think about the report due tomorrow or yesterday's missed opportunity; he's 100 per cent present in his calls.

I've seen salespeople increase productivity by 20–30 per cent within a month of implementing time blocking. The secret? Don't just block time for client-facing activities; do so for preparation, admin work and—yes—breaks!

FOCUS Goals: Your GPS for Time Management

If you don't know precisely where you're going, you'll waste time wandering. During my workshops, I teach a framework called FOCUS. In this framework, each goal should be **finite** (the goal must have clear boundaries and an end point), **outcome-oriented** (it should define a specific result you're aiming for), **challenging** (it must push you out of your comfort zone to encourage growth), **useful** (it must be relevant and add real value to your overall mission) and **scheduled** (it should be tied to a concrete timeline for completion).

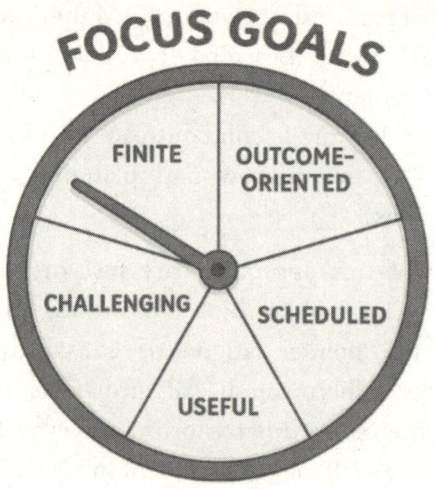

When I was at Maruti Suzuki, I noticed that salespeople with FOCUS goals consistently outperformed those with vague intentions. One rep went from middle-of-the-pack to top performer simply by replacing his ambiguous goal of 'grow my territory' with 'add three new dealerships in the eastern sector by 30 June'.

FOCUS goals eliminate the fatigue that comes from making a decision. Instead of constantly thinking about what deserves your attention, you've already mapped your priorities. This clarity alone can save you hours each week.

Automation: Your 24/7 Sales Assistant

Imagine having a tireless assistant who handles routine tasks while you focus on high-value activities. That's the power of automation.

During my time at ed-tech start-ups, I've seen salespeople transform their productivity with simple automation tools. For example:

- *CRM systems:* Salesforce, Zoho CRM or HubSpot can track customer interactions and set follow-up reminders automatically.
- *Email sequences:* Tools like MailChimp or ConvertKit send perfectly timed follow-ups without you lifting a finger.
- *Social media scheduling:* Hootsuite posts content across platforms when your audience is most active.
- *Meeting schedulers:* Calendly eliminates the back-and-forth email dance when setting appointments.

Even without fancy software, you can create simple automations. I taught my team to use Gmail filters to categorise incoming messages, Zapier to connect apps and Google Calendar for scheduling and reminders. Those tedious, repetitive actions in Quadrant 3 of your Eisenhower Matrix are best suited for automation.

Having seen the power of modern tools, I would like to mention Kamal Mahata from one of the dealerships of Maruti Suzuki in Delhi. While on my monthly review meeting with this dealership's team, I realised that Kamal did not have a single complaint from customers, and he continued to remain the highest-selling salesman too. Other members of the sales team had significant complaints in spite of fewer sales. Utterly surprising!

When I asked him about it, he showed me his diary in which each and every commitment to the customer was mentioned—test drive time, car delivery date promised, document collection, processing of finance, a special registration plate ... pretty much *anything*. Everything was documented in that diary, and he was managing his entire day prioritising customer commitments. No modern tools or apps, simple paper and pen.

No wonder he had zero complaints and the highest sales.

Delegation: The Multiplier Effect

The most valuable lesson I learnt as I moved from individual contributor to leadership roles was that trying to do everything yourself is the fastest path to mediocrity.

Many people—in the sales field or other professions—resist delegation because 'it's faster to do it myself' or 'nobody does it exactly how I like it'. But that's short-term thinking. Yes, delegation requires initial investment—explaining the task, checking work, providing feedback—but the long-term payoff is enormous.

What to delegate? Start with:

- *Administrative tasks:* CRM updates, data entry, scheduling
- *Research:* Basic company research, contact information gathering

- *Content customisation:* Adapting presentations or proposals using templates

When I led the team at Maruti Suzuki, one particular manager of a dealership was constantly missing his numbers despite working late every night. After analysing his workflow, we discovered that he spent nearly fifteen hours weekly on administrative tasks. Once he delegated these to a shared assistant, his team's sales jumped the very next quarter.

Remember: delegation isn't about dumping work on others; it's about maximising everyone's impact by matching tasks to the right skill sets.

TARGETS: Your Time Management Mantra

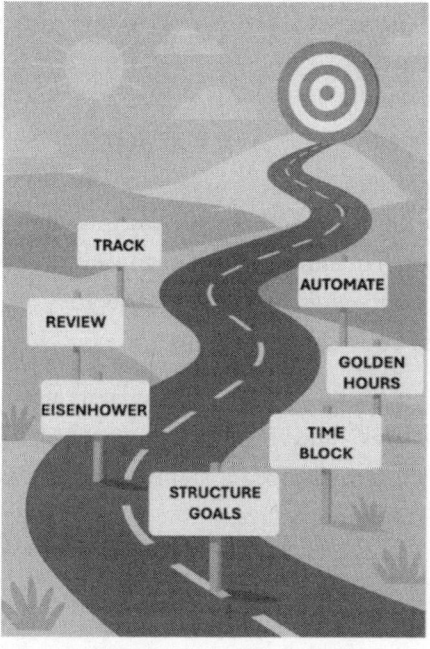

Let me give you a framework that brings all these concepts together—a mantra you can use daily to master your time. I call it TARGETS.

- *Track:* Monitor where you actually spend your time using apps like Toggl or even a simple spreadsheet. Most salespeople are shocked when they see the reality of their time allocation.
- *Automate:* Set up systems that handle repetitive tasks while you sleep. Even simple automations like email templates save hours weekly.
- *Review:* Schedule weekly reviews to assess what worked, what didn't, and adjust accordingly. This habit alone prevents weeks of wasted effort.
- *Golden hours:* Identify when your prospects are most responsive and protect those windows for direct outreach.
- *Eisenhower Matrix:* Ruthlessly prioritise using the four quadrants. If it's not important, why is it on your plate?
- *Time block:* Structure your day into focused segments rather than allowing it to become a reactive scramble.
- *Structure goals:* Set clear, specific objectives that guide your daily decisions.

I've taught this framework to hundreds of sales professionals across industries, and the results speak for themselves. Almost all of them showed a significant increase in closing rates within just ninety days.

Rohit's Final Thoughts

Time management isn't just about squeezing more work into each day; it's making sure the right work gets done at the right time. It's about being intentional rather than reactive.

As American educator Peter Drucker wisely said, 'Nothing is less productive than doing efficiently what shouldn't be done at all.'

True productivity isn't measured by exhaustion or hours worked but by results achieved. The best salespeople aren't necessarily working more hours; they're working the right hours on the right activities.

Remember: time is the only resource you can never get back. Invest it wisely, and watch your sales—and your life—transform.

My Final Two Cents

- *Prioritise ruthlessly:* Use the Eisenhower Matrix to focus on what truly matters, not just what's loudest.
- *Identify your golden hours:* Schedule high-value outreach when prospects are most likely to engage.
- *Block your time:* Create dedicated windows for different activities rather than multitasking.
- *Set FOCUS goals:* Replace vague intentions with finite, outcome-oriented objectives.
- *Automate the routine:* Let technology handle repetitive tasks while you focus on building relationships.
- *Delegate strategically:* Multiply your impact by focusing only on what requires your unique skills.

- *Review regularly:* Weekly assessment prevents small inefficiencies from becoming major time-wasters.

Time management isn't just another sales skill; it's the foundation that makes all other skills effective. Master it, and you'll not only sell more but you'll also enjoy the process far more.

STEP 6: MASTER THE CLOSE

Aapko kya laga? You identified a prospect, gave a fantastic demo and now you're just waiting for them to whip out their credit card? Oh, my friend, that's like expecting marriage after the first date!

I—Anand—have learnt (through my many failures) that the path from 'nice presentation' to 'where do I sign?' is paved with patience, persistence and a special kind of persuasion that doesn't make you sound like that overeager auntie trying to marry off her children at every family gathering.

Over the years, I've watched countless salespeople rush the close, and then wonder why their prospects ghosted them faster than a bad Tinder match. The reality? Most significant sales happen after at least five touchpoints. FIVE! Not one, not two—FIVE. This isn't what they teach you in those motivational 'become a sales shark' seminars where everyone high-fives and chants success mantras.

The Daily Discipline

If there's one habit that transformed my career, it's running through my 'Sales Saptarishi' (the seven sages of sales) every single morning. Picture me at my desk, coffee in hand, asking myself these seven questions:

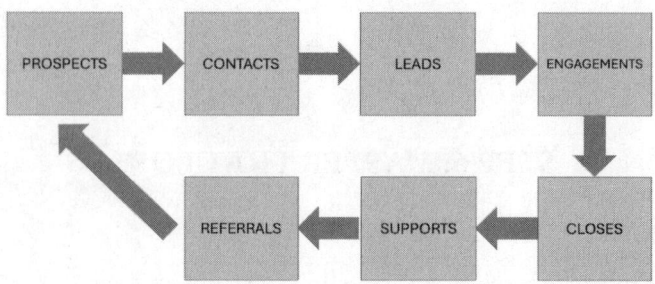

- *Prospects:* Which new potential customers can I add to my database today?
- *Contacts:* Which of those prospects should I reach out to today?
- *Leads:* Which contacts can I meet or do demonstrations for today?
- *Engagements:* Which leads need a follow-up or nudge today?
- *Closes:* Which engaged prospects am I ready to close today?
- *Supports:* Which recent customers need a post-sale touchpoint today?
- *Referrals:* Which satisfied customers could I approach for referrals today?

This daily ritual keeps your pipeline flowing like the Ganga—constant, powerful and life-giving. But I won't lie—maintaining this discipline requires the same mental fortitude as dragging yourself to the gym at 6 a.m. There are days when you'll want to skip it, days when you'll question if it's worth it. But just like those squats and deadlifts, this routine builds your sales muscles in ways nothing else can.

The Art of Persuasion without Pushiness

Early in my career, I was that annoying salesperson who wouldn't let customers breathe. When I was selling copper scrap and industrial materials, I hovered over potential buyers like a drone, bombarding them with specifications and discounts until they either bought something just to escape or fled the meeting entirely.

Then my sales manager, Praveen Mathur, took me aside and said something I'll never forget: 'Anand, you're selling to professionals, not hawking vegetables at a street market. Stop shouting about the price and start listening for the need.'

That advice changed everything. I learnt that persuasion isn't about talking someone into submission; it's about connecting with them and positioning your product as the solution they've been searching for.

The first rule of persuasion is respect. Think about how you feel when a salesperson trails you around a store, breathing down your neck with constant 'suggestions'. Annoying, right? That's exactly how your customers feel when you get pushy. Give them space. A simple 'I'm here if you need any help' often works better than a ten-minute feature demonstration they never asked for.

I remember watching an excellent electronics salesman handle an undecided customer at a store I was consulting with. The gentleman had been visiting the showroom for days, trying the same high-end camera repeatedly, but never committing. Instead of getting frustrated, this salesman would patiently answer the same questions, offer new perspectives on photography and, most importantly, never make the customer feel rushed. Eventually, not only did the customer buy the camera but he also referred two friends from his photography club and friends' circle who became customers.

The key was this salesman's calm, steady approach. He didn't need to be loud or aggressive. His confidence in the product and genuine interest in the customer's needs did the talking for him.

When persuasion seems to stall and the customer needs more time, the worst thing you can do is pile on more information or repeat your pitch (a mistake I've made more times than I care to admit). There's a fine line between explaining and annoying. The best move is to step back, and give them space to think. Let them know you'll follow up and then actually do it.

Instead of asking, 'How come you haven't made a decision yet?' (which sounds accusatory), try, 'Is there any specific information you're still looking for?' This puts you in the role of helper, not pusher.

Remember, this patient approach only works when you have a robust pipeline. If you're desperate for this one sale, you'll inevitably become pushy. That's why the daily Sales Saptarishi ritual is so crucial—it keeps you from putting all your eggs in one buyer's basket.

Crafting Win-Win Outcomes

Another big mistakes salespeople make is thinking of negotiation as haggling in a street market—whoever gives up less 'wins'. But most successful sales deals create winners on both sides.

Think about it this way: have you ever attended a satsang or listened to a spiritual pravachan? The message is always about finding *jeevan mein santulan*—balance in life—and cultivating *sadbhaav*—goodwill towards others. Apply this wisdom to your sales process, and magic happens.

During my time at Honda, we didn't just sell motorcycles; we created experiences where both sides walked away feeling they'd won. Customers who feel they've squeezed every last rupee of discount from you aren't victorious customers—they're often suspicious that they've missed something. Similarly, if you feel you've extracted every possible paisa from them, you haven't built a relationship; you've just completed a transaction.

A well-designed offer is more than discounts; it's about perceived value. It's that sweet spot where the customer feels they're getting something special, and you're building a long-term relationship.

Let me share a story that illustrates this perfectly. While carrying out research for a consulting assignment, I studied an electronics retailer's operations. One day, a tech-savvy professional came in looking for a high-end laptop. He loved the model but kept circling back to the price, comparing it with online competitors. Instead of jumping into a discount battle, their sales manager focused on what the customer really valued—expertise and support.

'Sir, I understand your concern about the price,' he said. 'What if we included our premium tech support package for a year? You'll have priority access to our certified technicians, remote troubleshooting and even data recovery services if needed. For someone who depends on their laptop professionally like yourself, how valuable would it be to have that level of support?'

The customer's eyes lit up. The conversation shifted from price to value. The store closed the deal that day, and he's referred several colleagues since then. And you know the best part? That support package cost the retailer far less than the discount the customer was initially pushing for.

Here are some win-win approaches I've seen work beautifully:

- *Software sales:* A free onboarding session costs the company little but dramatically increases customer success and loyalty.
- *Real estate:* Flexibility on closing dates or move-in times often matters more to buyers than a price reduction. I've seen deals close because a developer allowed early storage of furniture—at virtually no cost to them.
- *Luxury retail:* Including a small, complimentary item with a major purchase makes customers feel special, encouraging repeat business. At Rolex, they might include a premium watch case that

costs them ₹5,000 but feels like a ₹25,000-gift to the customer.
- *Automotive:* We offer a free annual detail and check-up that costs us relatively little but gives buyers tremendous peace of mind.

The principle is simple: find something that your customer values highly but doesn't cost you significantly. That's the sweet spot for a win-win.

One of my favourite examples of this comes from my cousin Shekhar, who is an insurance agent in Baroda. One of his prospective clients wanted health insurance but was worried about the upfront premium.

Instead of losing the sale, Shekhar offered quarterly instalments in place of a lump sum payment, and also included complimentary annual health check-ups. The customer got coverage within his budget constraints, and Shekhar secured a loyal customer who has since renewed multiple times and referred family members.

When done right, these approaches, along with closing the immediate sale, build the foundation for a long-term relationship.

The CAN Framework: Your Closing Secret Weapon

Now let's talk about a framework that has saved me in countless tough negotiations—CAN: Communicate, Assert, Negotiate. It's a three-step approach that helps you navigate those tricky moments when customers start hesitating or pushing back on price.

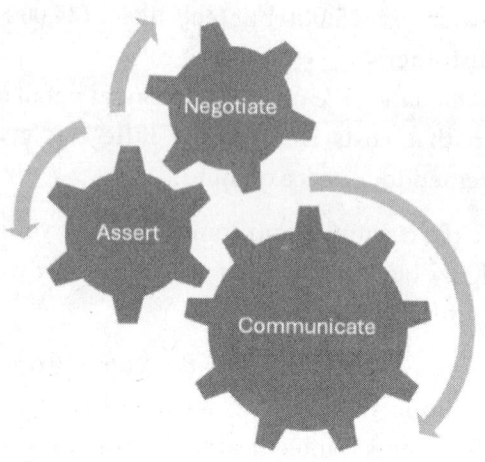

Communicate

The first step is positive engagement. Instead of launching into a rehearsed pitch, start with a question that invites the customer to share their thoughts.

During my years at Maruti Suzuki, I was once helping a public sector manager who was evaluating our premium hatchback. He and his family were circling the display car at a Mumbai dealership, checking features but not really engaging. The dealer salesman was about to launch into our standard feature presentation when I stepped in with: 'What kind of driving do you typically do as a family?'

That simple question opened the floodgates. The father shared that they took monthly road trips to visit grandparents in Pune, but their current car was uncomfortable for the kids on long journeys. Now we had a direction—we could focus our presentation on cabin space, entertainment options and fuel efficiency for long drives rather than generic features.

By starting with genuine questions, you accomplish two things: you make customers feel valued, and you gather intelligence that helps you tailor your approach.

Assert

Once you understand their needs, it's time to confidently present your solution—not aggressively, not apologetically, but with quiet assurance.

Continuing with the family, once I understood their road trip needs, I could assert with confidence: 'This model is perfect for family journeys. The adjustable rear seats give you 20 per cent more legroom than standard hatchbacks, while the integrated entertainment system keeps the kids engaged on long drives. Plus, the enhanced suspension provides a smoother ride on those bumpy highway stretches you mentioned.'

Notice I didn't say it's 'pretty good' or 'one of the better options'. I stated with conviction that it was perfect for their specific need. This isn't exaggeration if you truly believe it's the right fit. Your confidence becomes contagious.

Negotiate

Now comes the delicate part. If the customer expresses concern about price or hesitates to commit, don't immediately offer discounts or concessions. Instead, reinforce the value of the product and find creative ways to enhance the deal. You can also ask, 'What's holding you back?' Then address their concern directly, honestly and completely.

With our road-tripping family, when they mentioned the price, I didn't offer a discount immediately. Instead, I said, 'I understand your concern about the investment. The value of this model isn't just in getting from point A to B—it's in the peaceful journeys where the kids aren't constantly asking, "Are we there yet?" and you arrive at your parents' home refreshed instead of exhausted. What if we included the premium roadside assistance package for two years? You'll have complete peace of mind knowing that any hiccup during your monthly trips will be handled within minutes.'

This approach:

- Reinforced the specific value relevant to their situation.
- Offered something special that didn't require price reduction.
- Addressed their underlying concern for reliability on long trips.

The result? They purchased the car that weekend. That sale also resulted in relationships with several other public sector employees.

The magic of the CAN framework lies in placing the decision in the customer's hands while guiding them to see the unique benefits that will affect their lives personally. It's like asking your child if they'd prefer to do their homework before or after dinner—you're giving them control within parameters you've already set.

Here are some examples of how to respond to common customer statements using the CAN framework:

Customer Statement	Your Response	Purpose
'Hmm, so many choices!'	'Absolutely, it's like choosing the best dish from a buffet. Let's find the one that suits you best.'	Shows you value their choice, and are in it together.
'I need this for my photography hobby.'	'Then you'll love this camera—it's excellent in low light and has incredible resolution. What kind of photography do you enjoy most?'	Personalises the recommendation while inviting their input.
'Can't decide, really.'	'Totally understandable. If you had to pick one feature that's most important for your photography, what would it be?'	Guides their thought process, giving them ownership.
'The price is a bit high.'	'I understand; the quality and specialised features do make a difference. Many professional photographers who are our clients tell us that this camera pays for itself within months through the quality of work it helps them produce.'	Justifies value without immediate discounting.

My Closing Philosophy

After working on so many sales, I've come to a surprising conclusion: the best closes don't feel like closes at all. They feel like the natural next step in a conversation between two people who've figured out they can help each other.

In my early days, I thought closing was about clever techniques and pressure tactics. I'd use lines like 'If you sign today, I can throw in …' or 'This price is only good until the end of the week.' Sometimes they worked, but they often left buyers feeling manipulated rather than served. They didn't come back, and they certainly didn't refer others.

Now I see the end of the of the sales process differently. In fact, it's not the end at all; it's the beginning of a relationship. When done right, the customer leaves you feeling 'opened' to new possibilities, supported in their decision and confident in their choice.

Remember, the art of closing lies not only in presenting your offer effectively but also in knowing when to step back, respect the customer's space and provide reassurance. Each interaction should leave them feeling heard, respected and genuinely valued.

When closing becomes a collaborative, win-win experience, it can lead to a relationship that can last for years and span multiple purchases. And isn't that what truly successful selling is all about?

Anand's Takeaways

- *Build trust first; don't rush the close:* Allow time to build trust and rapport. A hurried close is usually a lost sale.
- *Practise daily discipline:* Run through the seven questions—prospect, contact, lead, engage, close, support, referral—every single day to keep your pipeline healthy.
- *Master persuasion without pushiness:* Stay calm, confident and patient. The most persuasive salespeople often say the least.
- *Create win-win outcomes:* Find the sweet spot where your customer gets exceptional value without costing you significant margins.
- *Use the CAN framework:* Communicate to understand needs, assert your solution confidently and negotiate with value-adds rather than discounts.
- *Welcome objections:* They're not roadblocks, they're signposts showing you exactly what needs to be addressed to move forward.
- *Remember that closing is opening:* When done right, closing a sale opens a long-lasting relationship with the customer.

My Parting Shot

There's an old saying in Indian sales: 'The customer is always right ... even when he's wrong, confused, broke and just came in for the free tea.'

Ravi, a senior sales manager for an industrial machine company, knew this better than anyone. Ravi was my college buddy and narrated this story to me many years later.

One day, a prospective client walked into his office, asking about a high-end packaging machine. Cost? About ₹40 lakh. It was a serious, B2B sale—the kind that could hit your entire monthly target.

The meeting started ... and *never ended.*

The customer asked a hundred questions.

Some reasonable: 'What is the speed per minute?'

Some philosophical: 'But in the larger sense, what *is* packaging?'

And some that Ravi still has nightmares about: 'Will your machine improve my family life?'

Ravi answered patiently. Every technical diagram. Every costing break-up. Once, during a particularly complicated explanation about conveyor belt torque, the client fell asleep at the table.

Ravi waited. Silently. For ten minutes, while the client snored gently.

When he finally woke up, he smiled and said, 'Good, good ... very reliable machine. Even your explanation lasted a long time—that's a good sign.'

The meeting continued. The client said he needed to 'confirm with family'—for an industrial machine, mind you, not a new sofa.

Ravi said, 'Of course, take your time.'

Six months passed. There were follow-up calls, site visits and more tea than Ravi had consumed in his entire life. Once, he even attended the client's nephew's birthday party because, apparently, 'building the relationship' was important.

Finally, the client called. 'Ravi-ji, some news! We have decided.'

Ravi held his breath.

The client said, 'We decided we are not expanding after all. My wife said the vaastu is not good for new machinery.'

Silence.

Ravi thanked him for considering their company, smiled and hung up.

Then he immediately called back. 'Sir, since expansion is not happening *right now*, should I block a meeting for next quarter? Just in case your vaastu consultant changes her mind?'

Because a real salesman knows that the client doesn't reject you. He just hasn't said 'yes' yet.

STEP 7: STAY ORGANISED

I, Rohit Goel, regional head of the country's largest automaker, recently met a sales guy from my network in his office. Let's just call him Hurricane Hari.

Bright eyes, endless energy and a desk that looked like a stationery store had exploded. Sticky notes were competing for space, three coffee cups were being used in rotation and I saw a to-do list that hadn't been touched since Monday ... of last week.

I pulled up a chair, smiled and said, 'Your drive is impressive. But chaos, my friend, doesn't close deals. If your desk, your day and your mind are all over the place, so will be your results.'

He blinked. Curious. Caught. He gave a sheepish grin—the kind that says, *I know you're right, but I don't know where to start.*

That conversation—simple as it was—turned out to be a quiet wake-up call. One that I think he really needed. Organisation isn't just some corporate buzzword or a 'Type A' personality trait. In sales, it's the invisible force that separates the struggling from the successful. Having trained hundreds of them, and I can tell you that well-organised salespeople aren't just more productive; they're more confident, more responsive and, ultimately, more trusted by their clients.

Let me show you how to transform from chaos to control without losing your sanity.

Your Workspace: The Command Centre

Your workspace—whether it's a corporate desk, home office or the passenger seat of your car—is your personal command centre. And just like a pilot better have a clean cockpit to fly safely, you need an organised space to sell effectively.

During my years in the automobile industry, I made it a point to visit our top salespeople across regions. One pattern became shockingly clear: our highest performers all maintained meticulous workspaces. Not necessarily spotless or Pinterest-worthy, but functionally organised.

Here's what I learnt from them regarding physical workspace essentials:

- *Keep it minimal:* Only items you use daily deserve desktop real estate. Everything else should have an assigned drawer or shelf.
- *Create zones:* Designate specific areas for different activities—a calling zone with a headset and notes, a meeting zone with presentation materials and a planning zone with your calendar and planner.
- *Maintain a 'today folder':* Keep a single folder or tray for everything you need for today's meetings and calls. Nothing more, nothing less.

When I was consulting with corporates, I once met a salesperson in Mumbai who carried a single leather portfolio with colour-coded tabs for each client meeting scheduled that day. While colleagues fumbled with overflowing bags, she smoothly transitioned between meetings, pulling out exactly what she needed within seconds. Her simple system helped her close 25 per cent more deals than her teammates.

Equally important are your digital workspace must-haves:

- *File naming conventions:* Searching for 'Satish proposal final FINAL actually final v3.docx' isn't fun. Develop a consistent naming system like 'ClientName_ProjectType_Date.'
- *Folder structure:* Create logical hierarchy with client-specific folders and sub-folders for proposals, contracts and communications.
- *Clean your digital desktop:* Just like your physical desk, your computer's desktop should be a functional space, not a dumping ground for every document you've created since 2015.

I personally use the '3-3-3 Rule': if I haven't opened a file in three days, it goes into a folder. If I haven't opened a folder in three weeks, it gets archived. If I haven't needed an archived folder in three months, it gets backed up and removed from my main drive.

When your workspace is organised, your mind is clearer, your responses are faster and it will show in your results.

Pipeline Management: Your Daily Bread

Remember the Sales Saptarishi that Anand mentioned in the previous chapter? That daily ritual of running through these seven questions is the heartbeat of organisation:

- *Prospect:* Which new prospects can I add to my database today?
- *Contact:* Which prospects should I reach out to today?
- *Lead:* Which contacts can I meet or demo today?
- *Engage*: Which leads need a follow-up today?
- *Close:* Which engaged prospects am I ready to close today?
- *Support:* Which customers need a post-sale touchpoint today?
- *Referral:* Which satisfied customers could I approach for referrals?

I had instituted a system called 'Morning Pipeline Mastery'—fifteen minutes every morning where the entire sales team would silently run through these questions and update their CRM accordingly. Within three months, our team's conversion rates improved by 15 per cent.

The magic happens when you segment your pipeline properly. Think of it like organising spices in your kitchen—when everything has its place, cooking becomes effortless.

Here's how to label your prospects effectively:

- *Use stage labels:* 'New lead', 'Contacted', 'Demo scheduled', 'Proposal sent,' 'Negotiation,' 'Closed won/lost'
- *Add timing tags:* 'Follow up today,' 'Follow up this week', 'Long-term nurture'
- *Include value indicators:* 'High value', 'Quick win', 'Strategic account'

I remember working with a struggling sales head at a General Motors dealership who complained that he was 'drowning in leads'. When we examined his system, I discovered why—he had one giant list labelled 'Prospects' with over 300 names, with no way to know who needed attention today versus next month. We spent one afternoon segmenting his pipeline, and within two weeks, his productivity doubled—simply because he knew exactly whom to focus on each day.

Pro tip: most modern CRMs let you create automated workflows where tasks and reminders are generated automatically when you move a prospect from one stage to another. This means less manual work and fewer things falling through the cracks.

Batch Similar Prospecting Activities Together

Prospecting without organisation is like fishing without a net—you might catch something, but you'll waste a lot of energy in the process.

When I was transforming my sales team at an agri-products company, I implemented a system called Batch Prospecting that revolutionised our team's results. The concept is simple but powerful:

- *Research batching:* Dedicate one to two hours twice weekly to research new prospects (I prefer Tuesday/Thursday mornings).
- *Outreach batching:* Block one to two hours for cold calls and initial emails (best during industry 'golden hours' when people are most responsive).
- *Follow-up batching:* Schedule thirty to sixty minutes daily for follow-up communications.

Why does this work so well? Because your brain performs better when it stays in one mode rather than constantly switching gears. When you're in 'research mode', you can dive deep and find quality prospects more efficiently. When you're in 'calling mode', you build momentum with each call.

Script and Template Libraries Are Another Game Changer

I maintain a digital collection of templates for every situation.

- Introduction emails
- Follow-up messages (first, second and third attempt variations)
- Meeting request templates
- Thank-you notes
- Objection-handling responses

Each template has customisable fields that I can quickly adapt to the specific prospect. This approach saves hours of typing while ensuring my messaging stays consistent.

One of our sales team leaders at a previous company created a brilliant system for organising his team's cold-calling efforts. He used a simple spreadsheet with colour-coding:

- Green: Ready to call (researched and prepared)
- Yellow: Need more research
- Blue: Called, left message, follow-up on (date)
- Red: Called, not interested
- Purple: Called, interested, next step scheduled

This visual system gave him an instant snapshot of his prospecting efforts and helped him maintain momentum throughout the week.

Meeting and Demo Prep That Impresses

Nothing kills your credibility faster than a disorganised meeting or demo. I've seen potential deals worth crores evaporate because a salesperson couldn't find a critical document or had technical issues with their presentation.

The secret to flawless meetings is having a pre-meeting checklist. I use a system I call The 5 Ps of Meeting Prep: Purpose, People, Points, Preparation, Post-meeting.

I keep a laminated copy of this checklist in my meeting folder and run through it before every client interaction.

My most valuable organisation hack for meetings is the immediate capture rule. Within five minutes of ending any client meeting, I record three things:

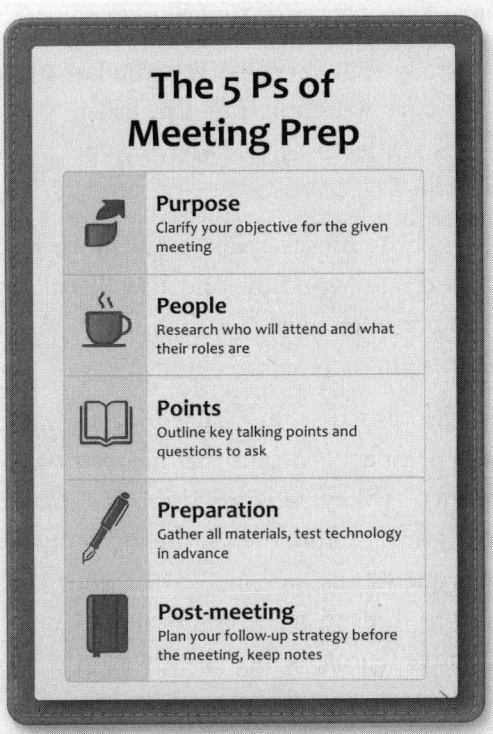

1. Key decisions or agreements made
2. Questions that need answering
3. Specific next steps with deadlines.

I don't trust my memory—and neither should you. Five minutes of documentation saves hours of confusion later. I often used the voice memo feature on my phone to record these notes while walking to my car after meetings. By the time I reach the office, I can quickly transcribe them into my CRM.

Technology: Your Organisation Superpower

I'm not naturally tech-savvy—I was the last person in my office to get a smartphone. But I've learnt that the right technology, used effectively, is like having a personal assistant working for you 24/7.

You don't need the most sophisticated tools; just find the right tools for *your* workflow and use them consistently. Here are my personal favourites that have transformed my sales organisation:

- *Trello:* I use this for visual pipeline management. Each prospect is a card that moves from one list to another as they progress through my sales funnel. The visual nature helps me instantly see where everyone stands.
- *Google Calendar:* Colour-coded for different activities (prospecting in green, client meetings in blue, internal meetings in yellow). I block time for specific activities rather than just scheduling meetings.
- *Evernote:* My second brain. I create a note for each client with every interaction, preference and detail logged chronologically. The search function lets me instantly find information from conversations from years ago.
- *Zoom with Calendly integration:* Clients can schedule time on my calendar based on my availability, and meeting links are automatically generated. This eliminates the endless email chains of 'How about

Tuesday at 2?' and 'No, I'm busy then. How about Wednesday?'
- *CRM (I've used both Salesforce and HubSpot):* The central database for all client information, interaction history and future tasks. The mobile app means I can update information immediately after meetings.

There are literally hundreds of tools that can make you more organised—apps like Evernote, Notion, OneNote, Google Keep and Apple Notes for capturing ideas; Todoist, Reminders and Google Tasks for managing to-do lists; iOS Calendar and Google Calendar for scheduling; OneDrive, Dropbox, Google Drive for storing documents; CamScanner and Adobe Scan for turning your phone into a portable scanner; Trello, Airtable, Slack for project and team management; HubSpot CRM, Pipedrive, Salesforce Mobile, Close CRM, Zoho CRM, Freshsales, LeadSquared, Odoo CRM for sales tracking; Toggl for time management; Calendly for scheduling meetings; Mailchimp for client engagement; SurveyMonkey for feedback; LinkedIn Sales Navigator and Apollo.io for lead generation; and even classics like Microsoft Excel and Google Sheets for flexible data organisation.

But here's the truth: *it's not the tool that matters; it's how you use it.* We've seen executives work wonders with just a paper diary and a mobile phone, while others armed with the latest technology still struggle. In the end, no tool can replace consistency, discipline and follow-through. It's easy to get overwhelmed or fall into the trap of thinking you need every shiny new tool that comes along. I've seen sales teams implement five different tools and end up less organised than when they started! The best system isn't the most advanced one; it's the one you'll actually use consistently. Don't get caught up in tool fatigue. Pick a few core solutions that address your specific pain points, master them thoroughly and stick with them long enough to build habits around them.

I once worked with a sales team that invested in an expensive CRM system but saw zero improvement in results. Why? Because they treated it like a reporting tool for management rather than a personal organisation system. They would call prospects, have meetings and then batch-update the CRM once a week. By then, details were forgotten, and follow-ups were missed. The system was only as good as the habits around it.

Post-Sale Organisation: Where Loyalty Is Born

As we mentioned in the previous chapter, the signing on the dotted line isn't the end of the deal; it's the beginning of the real relationship. Organised post-sale engagement sets you up for renewals, upsells, cross-sells and those golden referrals.

I remember implementing the 30–90–180 system for every new customer:

- *30 days:* Check-in call to ensure satisfaction and address any initial concerns
- *90 days:* More in-depth review of their experience and identification of any new needs

- *180 days:* Comprehensive satisfaction review and introduction of complementary products/services.

Each of these touchpoints is automatically scheduled in our CRM the moment a sale is closed, with specific templates and talking points prepared in advance.

Document Key Material about Your Customers

I can tell you this with confidence because it helped me win a crucial deal.

During an early conversation, a client casually mentioned that his daughter was applying to medical schools. I noted it down in. Weeks later, during a follow-up call, I simply asked, 'How's your daughter's application process going?'

He paused—pleasantly surprised—and said, 'You remembered that?' That small moment of connection shifted the tone entirely. It moved the relationship from transactional to trusted.

We closed the deal not just because of pricing or product but because we cared enough to remember. Today, my client file includes:

- Personal preferences (communication style, best time to contact)
- Key dates (contract renewals, company fiscal year)
- Personal notes (family mentions, hobbies, alma mater)
- Previous pain points and how they were resolved.

Discipline in documentation isn't admin work, it's relationship work. And in sales, relationships win. This information is gold for personalised service that builds unshakeable loyalty.

Personal Routines: The Foundation of Organisation

Organisation isn't about tools or systems; it's about habits. The most powerful organisational tool isn't a fancy CRM; it's consistent, daily routines that keep you on track. For example, here's my Morning Power Routine (fifteen minutes):

- Review the day's calendar and identify the three most important outcomes
- Run through the Sales Saptarishi questions
- Prepare materials for the day's first appointments
- Take a moment to visualise successful interactions.

I've been starting my day this way for over fifteen years, whether I'm in a corporate office or working from a hotel room while travelling. This routine centres me and ensures I never miss critical follow-ups. Similarly, there's my Friday Wrap-up (twenty minutes):

- Review the week's wins and challenges
- Clean up my CRM and ensure all interactions are documented
- Identify the top priorities for next week
- Schedule specific time blocks for next week's key activities.

This weekly review prevents small oversights from becoming major issues and helps me start Monday with clarity and purpose.

One sales manager I coached had a brilliant personal routine—he set aside the first thirty minutes after lunch each day for 'tying up loose ends'. This was dedicated time to handle any unexpected issues that came up in the morning, ensure all meeting notes were properly filed and prepare for afternoon appointments. This midday reset kept him from falling behind as the day progressed.

Real-World Organisation Success

Let me tell you about Keshav, a key accounts manager I mentored at an agri-tech company. When we first met, he was struggling—missing follow-ups, losing documents and generally overwhelmed by his workload despite working twelve-hour days.

We implemented a simple organisation system:

- *Morning planning ritual:* Fifteen minutes to review and prioritise the day's activities
- *Contact segmentation:* Categorising leads based on stage and potential value
- *Task batching:* Grouping similar activities (calls, emails, proposals) into dedicated time blocks
- *End-of-day documentation:* Ten minutes to update his CRM and prepare for the next day.

Within six weeks, Keshav was working fewer hours but closing more sales. His conversion rate increased by a third, and clients began specifically requesting to work with him because of his responsiveness and reliability.

The most telling feedback came from his manager: 'It's like we hired a completely different person—in the best possible way.'

The Bottom Line on Organisation

Organisation isn't glamorous. It doesn't have the adrenaline rush of closing a big deal or the dopamine hit of seeing a new lead come in. But it's the foundation that makes everything else possible.

When I look back at my career journey, the turning point wasn't when I mastered my pitch or developed better product knowledge; it was when I got organised.

Organisation gives you the freedom to focus on what truly matters: building relationships and solving problems for your customers. When you're not constantly searching for information or playing catch-up with overdue tasks, you can be fully present in every interaction.

Start small. Pick one area to organise this week—it could be your workspace, your digital files or your follow-up system. Master that, and then move to the next. Organisation is built through consistent small improvements, not overnight transformations.

Remember: in sales, your product isn't the only thing being evaluated. Your professionalism, reliability and attention to detail are equally important to customers—and organisation is how those qualities shine through.

Chalo, to Sum Up ...

- *Create command centre workspaces:* Organise both physical and digital workspaces for distraction-free focus and quick access to what you need, when you need it.
- *Pipeline with purpose:* Use the Sales Saptarishi questions daily, and segment your contacts to ensure no opportunity falls through the cracks.
- *Batch similar activities:* Group prospecting, calling and follow-up tasks into dedicated time blocks to maintain focus and build momentum.
- *Prepare methodically for meetings:* Use checklists to ensure nothing is missed, and document key points immediately after each interaction.
- *Leverage technology wisely:* Find tools that fit your workflow, but remember that technology only amplifies your existing habits, good or bad.
- *Nurture post-sale relationships systematically:* Schedule regular check-ins and maintain detailed records of customer preferences and history.
- *Establish personal routines:* Create consistent daily and weekly habits that keep you organised without requiring constant willpower.

Organisation doesn't mean you have to be perfect; you just need to create systems that work for you and not against you. Master it, and watch your sales deals transform from chaos to consistent success.

STEP 8: NURTURE YOUR RELATIONSHIPS

Let me share a painful lesson that I, Anand Prakash, learnt early in my career.

I was working at Sterling Copper, hitting my targets, closing deals like a champion—but something strange was happening. My sales would spike for a month, then plummet the next. It was like riding a roller coaster blindfolded.

One day, my mentor pulled me aside and asked, 'Anand, when was the last time you called a customer after selling to them?'

I stared blankly. 'Why would I call them? All the sales formalities are over.'

He laughed, not unkindly. 'That's why you're struggling. You're treating customers like one-night stands instead of marriages.'

Crude? Perhaps. But it was the wake-up call I needed.

In this industry, a transaction isn't just an exchange of goods or services. It's the beginning of a relationship. Think about it: would you rather walk into a store where the salesperson greets you by name and remembers your preferences, or one where you're treated like a walking wallet? The personal connection makes all the difference.

The hard numbers back this up. Acquiring a new customer costs five to seven times more than retaining an existing one. Research from Bain & Company shows that increasing customer retention by just 5 per cent can boost profits by minimum 25 per cent. And loyal customers spend roughly 67 per cent more than new ones.

But beyond the statistics, there's a simple human truth: we all want to feel valued. When we do, we come back. We tell our friends. We become advocates. In today's world of endless options and minimal product differentiation, the relationship you build often becomes the deciding factor.

So how do you transform transactional interactions into meaningful relationships? Let me show you.

The RELATE Framework: Your Relationship Blueprint

I've developed a framework for building customer relationships called RELATE. There are six elements in this framework: Respect, Engage, Listen, Adapt, Trust and Empathise.

Respect Their Intelligence

Years ago, when I was selling Honda motorcycles, a customer asked my colleague about mileage on a sports bike. He snickered and replied, 'Sir, it's a sports bike, not an autorickshaw. Nobody buys it for the mileage.'

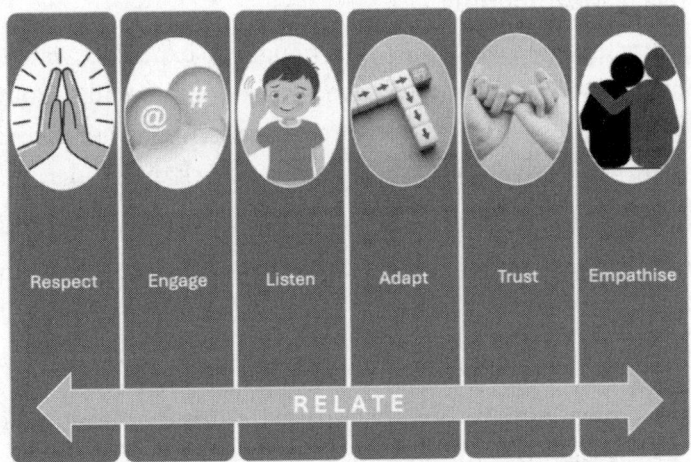

The customer quietly left and, we learnt later, bought from our competitor.

The lesson? Every question deserves respect—even the ones that seem trivial to you. What might seem like a basic question to an expert like you represents a genuine concern for your customer.

Showing respect means:

- Answering every question patiently, no matter how basic
- Acknowledging their expertise in their own field
- Never making them feel foolish for asking.

Remember: your customer isn't stupid—they're just not an expert in your product. And they shouldn't have to be.

Engage Meaningfully

Picture this scenario: you've just bought an expensive watch. The next day, you receive five promotional emails about other watches. The day after, three more arrive in your inbox. By the end of the week, you're ready to block the sender.

Sound familiar? This is engagement without meaning—noise that pushes customers away rather than pulling them closer.

Meaningful engagement means connecting with purpose:

- Send information that's useful, not just promotional
- Reach out through their preferred channels (some prefer WhatsApp, others email)
- Time your communications thoughtfully—not too frequent, not too sparse.

I've found that the sweet spot is reaching out once every two to three weeks with something genuinely valuable—whether it's usage tips, relevant industry news or a personalised offer based on their past purchases.

Remember the adage, Out of sight, out of mind? For sales, I add: 'In sight too often, out of patience.'

Listen Actively

At Maruti Suzuki, I worked with a dealership sales executive named Parag who had an uncanny ability to remember everything a customer said—not just about cars but about their lives, families and concerns.

It wasn't a superhuman skill. His secret was that he actually listened.

Most salespeople aren't listening; they're just waiting for their turn to speak. They hear the words but miss the meaning. True listening is about understanding the customer's underlying needs, not just their stated requirements.

Try these listening techniques:

- Ask open-ended questions like 'What challenges are you facing with your current solution?'
- Repeat what you've heard to confirm understanding.
- Notice non-verbal cues—sometimes what they don't say tells you more than what they do.

I once had a customer who kept asking about the durability of a certain material. I could have just quoted specifications, but by listening closely, I realised he was actually concerned about his children damaging the product. This insight allowed me to address his real concern: peace of mind, not technical specs.

Adapt Your Approach

Does one size fit all? Maybe for cheap T-shirts but definitely not for customer relationships.

Customers broadly fall into four communication styles, and we have to tailor our conversations with them accordingly:

- *The Direct:* They want facts, figures, and efficiency
- *The Analytical:* They need details, data and demonstrations

- *The Expressive:* They respond to stories, enthusiasm and the big picture
- *The Amiable:* They value personal connection, reassurance and harmony.

Your job is to spot which type you're dealing with and adapt accordingly. When I'm speaking with a Direct type, I keep my communication brief and to the point. With an Analytical customer, I come prepared with specific data and detailed answers.

Adaptation isn't manipulation; it's meeting customers where they are, speaking their language and making them comfortable.

Trust through Transparency

I was managing automotive sales in 2008 when the economic downturn began to affect all industries. Supply chain issues hit us hard, and delivery times doubled overnight.

We had two choices: be vague about delivery timelines (hoping things would improve) or be transparent about the delays.

We chose transparency. We called every customer, explained the situation and offered options: wait with a small compensation for the delay, or cancel their order with no penalty.

Surprisingly, 85 per cent chose to wait. Why? Because our honesty built trust. Trust is the foundation of any lasting relationship, and transparency is how you build it:

- Be honest about what your product can and cannot do
- When problems arise, communicate quickly and clearly
- Never overpromise just to make a sale.

One transparent conversation is worth a hundred marketing messages.

Empathise Genuinely

When a customer is frustrated, their emotions often speak louder than their words. Recognising and acknowledging them is empathy.

I remember a customer who was furious about a delayed delivery. Instead of becoming defensive or offering excuses, I simply said, 'I understand this is frustrating. If I were in your position, I'd be upset too. Let's figure out how we can make this right.'

The tension dissolved immediately. He still wanted his issue resolved, but the emotional temperature dropped significantly.

Empathy statements that work:

- 'I understand how frustrating this must be ...'
- 'I can see why this would be concerning ...'
- 'You have every right to be disappointed ...'

Empathy doesn't mean you have to fix everything immediately. Sometimes, people just need to know they've been heard and understood.

Making Interactions Personal: Small Touches, Big Impact

Have you ever walked into your favourite chai shop and had the owner greet you by name, remembering exactly how you like your tea? How did that make you feel? Special, right?

That's the power of personalisation.

When a customer returns to your store after showing interest a week earlier, what should you do? Simple. Remember them. Their name, their needs, their previous queries. Few things make a customer feel more valued than a salesperson who remembers them.

In the past, I have trained sales personnel to use a simple system that makes this easy:

- After each customer interaction, note three key details in your CRM
- When they return, quickly review these notes before approaching them
- Reference previous conversations naturally: 'Last time you mentioned you were looking for something with extra legroom. I've found a few options that might work perfectly for you.'

This isn't rocket science, but it's remarkable how few salespeople actually do it. Most treat returning customers like complete strangers—and miss a golden opportunity to deepen the relationship.

Beyond remembering details, here are some personalisation techniques that have worked wonders for my teams:

- *Celebration outreach:* Acknowledge purchase anniversaries with a simple message: 'It's been one year since you purchased your laptop! How has your experience been?' These timely check-ins show you're thinking about them beyond the sale.
- *Preference tracking:* Note communication preferences (email vs. WhatsApp), best times to call and personal interests. One of my salespeople noticed a customer was interested in cricket and sent him a message when we sponsored a local tournament. That small gesture led to two referral sales.
- *Customised recommendations:* Instead of sending generic promotional material, tailor your suggestions based on previous purchases and expressed interests.

Proven Techniques That Worked for Me

A personalised experience transforms a transaction into a relationship. And in today's world of automated messages and chatbots, the human touch stands out more than ever. One of the goals of all salespersons is customer retention. But retention isn't just about keeping customers, it's also about growing them. Here are proven techniques that have dramatically increased customer lifetime value for my businesses.

Segment Your Customers (Not All Are Created Equal)

Not all customers need the same level of attention. That might sound harsh, but it's a reality of limited time and resources. At an electronics outfit I consulted, I observed they segment customer base into tiers:

- *Platinum:* High-value, multiple purchases, active referrers
- *Gold:* Regular purchasers with growth potential
- *Silver:* Occasional buyers
- *Bronze:* One-time purchasers.

Each tier receives different communication frequency, perks and personal attention. Platinum customers get quarterly personal check-ins from senior staff, while bronze might receive automated seasonal greetings with incentives to re-engage.

This isn't about neglecting certain customers; it's about allocating resources where they'll have the greatest impact.

Anticipate Needs (Before They Know They Have Them)

A reactive salesperson responds to customer requests. A proactive one anticipates their needs. For instance, when someone buys their first car, the salesman should know from experience they'll likely have questions about maintenance around the three-month mark. Instead of waiting for them to call with concerns, he should reach out first: 'Many of our first-time car owners have questions about proper maintenance at this stage. Would you like me to walk you through what to expect?'

This proactive approach positions you as a partner in their success, not just a vendor who disappears after the sale.

Use Emotional Intelligence (EQ) to Read between the Lines

A customer who says 'I'm just looking' might really mean:

- 'I don't want to be pressured.'
- 'I'm not sure you have what I need.'
- 'I've had bad experiences with salespeople before.'

High EQ allows you to detect these underlying concerns and address them appropriately. If someone seems hesitant about a high-end product, don't immediately jump to discussing financing options. Instead, focus on value and long-term benefits.

Match your energy to theirs. If they're reserved, be calm and measured. If they're enthusiastic, mirror that excitement. This emotional adjustment creates rapport at a subconscious level.

Create Feedback Loops That Actually Improve Your Service

Many businesses collect feedback but do nothing with it. The real power comes from closing the loop:

- Collect specific feedback
- Make improvements based on that feedback
- Tell customers what you changed because of their input.

When customers see their suggestions implemented, they feel invested in your success. They become partners, not just purchasers.

Here's a simple approach I use. After implementing a change based on customer feedback, I personally call the customers who suggested it and say, 'Remember that suggestion you made? We've implemented it. I'd love to get your thoughts on how it's working.'

This call often leads to deeper engagement and, frequently, additional sales.

Recover From Mistakes with Grace (Turn Complainers into Advocates)

Every business makes mistakes. The difference between those that retain customers and those that lose them is how they handle the recovery. When things go wrong, follow this four-step process:

- Acknowledge the issue without excuses
- Apologise sincerely
- Fix the problem promptly
- Offer something extra to compensate for the inconvenience.

I'll share a personal story. One of our sales associates accidentally sent a customer the wrong accessory package for their new car. When we discovered the error, I personally delivered the correct package to the customer's home, along with a complimentary detailing service voucher.

That customer has since referred five friends to our company—more than many of our satisfied customers. Why? Because when things go wrong, we have the opportunity to demonstrate our values in action.

Leveraging Technology Without Losing the Human Touch

Technology can help you scale personalisation—if used correctly. Here's how we use tech tools while keeping relationships human:

CRM Systems: Your Relationship Memory Bank

A good CRM isn't just for tracking sales; it's for remembering the human details that build connections. In our CRM, beyond the usual purchase details, we record:

- Family milestones mentioned in conversation (children's graduations, upcoming weddings)
- Personal interests and hobbies
- Communication preferences
- Past concerns or service issues
- Specific compliments they've given about products or service.

These details allow any team member to pick up a conversation naturally, even if they weren't part of previous interactions.

Social Listening: Understanding What Matters to Them

Tools like Hootsuite or Brandwatch help you monitor what customers are saying online. Don't look at this as stalking; you're understanding their changing needs and interests.

For instance, if several customers in the same industry are discussing a new regulatory challenge on LinkedIn, that's an opportunity to reach out with relevant solutions or information.

Balancing Automation and Personalisation

Automation can handle routine communications, freeing you to focus on high-value personal interactions. We use a '70/30 rule':

- Seventy per cent of communications can be templated but personalised (using their name and relevant details).
- Thirty per cent should be completely customised and personal.

Even with automated messages, we build in mechanisms for personal follow-up. For example, our system sends automated purchase anniversary emails, but if a customer responds, a real person continues the conversation.

The goal isn't to eliminate human interaction; it's to enhance it by handling routine communications efficiently.

The Rajdhani Restaurant Bell: Simple Ideas That Work

Sometimes the most effective relationship-building tools are surprisingly simple.

I love the story of Rajdhani, a Gujarati thali restaurant in Ahmedabad. Nearly two decades ago, long before anyone talked about Net Promoter Scores, they placed a bell at their exit with a sign reading, 'If you are happy with us, please ring the bell.'

When a customer rang it, the entire staff would call out 'Aavjo!'—meaning 'Thank you, please come again!' If a customer didn't ring the bell, a manager would immediately ask, 'How can we improve?'

This simple system accomplished several things:
- It gave immediate feedback
- It created a moment of connection between the staff and satisfied customers
- It immediately identified improvement opportunities
- It made customers feel their opinion mattered.

What's your equivalent of the Rajdhani bell? What simple mechanism could you create to strengthen connections with your customers?

The CUSTOMER Framework: Your Relationship Checklist

To bring all these concepts together, I use the CUSTOMER framework as a daily reminder of relationship essentials:

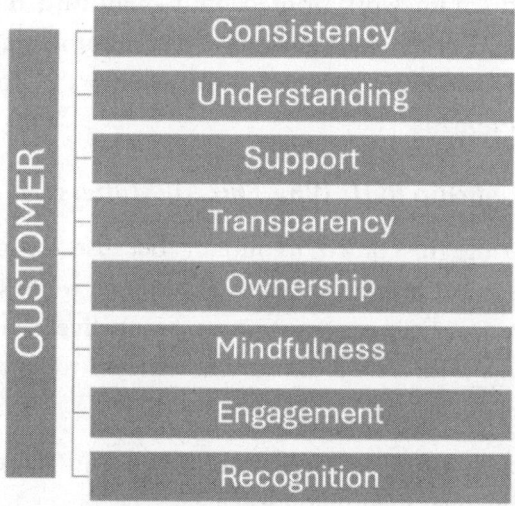

What is involved in reviewing these essentials?

- *Consistency:* Maintain regular, predictable contact.
- *Understanding*: Know their pain points and preferences.
- *Support:* Offer help proactively, not just reactively.
- *Transparency:* Be honest about capabilities and limitations.
- *Ownership:* Take responsibility when things go wrong.
- *Mindfulness:* Stay present and focused during interactions.
- *Engagement:* Create two-way conversations, not monologues.
- *Recognition:* Acknowledge loyalty and make them feel valued.

I've had this framework printed on a small card that sits on my desk. Before any significant customer interaction, I glance at it as a reminder of what truly matters in building lasting relationships.

The Relationship ROI: Why This All Matters

Let me bring this down to money because, ultimately, business is about results. At my establishment, we measured the difference between customers we actively nurture relationships with versus those who receive the standard follow-up:

- Relationship-nurtured customers spend 70 per cent more over their lifetime

- They refer 3x more new customers
- They're 4x less likely to switch to competitors when offered discounts
- Their satisfaction scores average 30 per cent higher.

These aren't small differences; they're business-transforming metrics that directly impact your bottom line.

Beyond the numbers, there's something deeply fulfilling about building genuine human connections with customers. In a world increasingly defined by automation and digital distance, being someone who truly cares about people—not just purchasers—is what sets you apart.

I began this chapter with a painful lesson from the early days of my career. Let me close it with the positive side of that same coin.

Relationship-building has always been my strength. I've never seen relationships as mere transactions. My approach is simple: be yourself, be honest and trust that everything else will follow. The relationships I formed at Honda and Maruti Suzuki still endure. In a world where people often forget you the moment you leave a position, I consider myself fortunate because many of my former dealer partners have become close friends—like family, really.

In fact, my entrepreneurial transition is itself the result of a relationship. When I was contemplating leaving a comfortable corporate job to strike out on my own, a senior Maruti Suzuki dealer said to me, 'Why don't you start a business with my son? I've seen you over the years, and I know my son won't find a better partner.' That gesture—

whether or not the deal would materialise—gave me the confidence to take that bold leap into entrepreneurship. The trust he placed in me was the fuel I needed.

Even this book—a dream project for me—was born out of long-standing relationships with Ashwin and Rohit, friendships that go back over fifteen years.

Or take another example. In 2019, when we launched our BMW dealership, our very first customer was a high-profile businessman, one Mr Arora. Unfortunately, he wasn't happy with the delivery experience and had a few issues with the product too. He was furious and gave my CEO (coincidentally, another Mr Arora) quite an earful, saying he regretted buying from a rookie dealership.

The very next morning, I personally went to Mr Arora's house, a small gift in hand—accompanied by my sales executive. He didn't know I was the owner. I apologised unconditionally and assured him we'd resolve everything. Within a few days, we addressed all his concerns to his full satisfaction.

Today, he's not just a repeat customer—having bought three more cars from us—but also a family friend. Over dinner one evening, he told me, 'Anand, you helped me when I had an issue and treated me like a friend, not a customer.'

There are countless such stories in my life. The lesson? Relationships aren't just 'nice to have'—they're investments. And like the best investments, they compound over time in ways you can't always predict. Every interaction is a deposit in the relationship bank. Make enough of them, and the returns will astonish you.

What It All Comes Down To

- *Trust is your foundation:* Build it through respect, transparency and consistent follow-through on promises.
- *Personalisation creates connection:* Remember details, customise interactions and make customers feel uniquely valued.
- *Technology enhances, does not replace:* Use CRMs and automation to scale personalisation, not eliminate it.
- *Recovery is an opportunity:* How you handle mistakes often leaves a stronger impression than flawless service.
- *Consistency builds confidence:* Regular, meaningful touchpoints create a sense of reliability that customers value.
- *Think long-term:* View each customer interaction as part of an ongoing relationship, not as a one-time transaction.
- *Small gestures yield big returns:* Thank-you notes, remembering preferences and timely check-ins create disproportionate loyalty.

Remember, in a world where products become increasingly similar, your relationship with the customer is often your only true competitive advantage. Nurture it like the precious asset it is.

STEP 9: DEVELOP A 24X7 MINDSET

Remember Citibank's classic tagline? 'Citi Never Sleeps.' That wasn't just clever marketing; it was a philosophy that revolutionised banking. And as someone who's spent over twenty-five years in sales leadership across several companies, now wiser and more experienced Rohit Goel can tell you that the best salespeople operate with the same philosophy.

Now, before you panic and picture yourself answering sales calls at 3 a.m. while your family disowns you, let me clarify. A 24x7 mindset doesn't mean working around the clock until you collapse from exhaustion. It means developing a perpetual awareness—a sales radar that's always scanning, even when you're officially 'off duty'.

In the past twenty-seven years working in industries as diverse as cement, automobile, education, social service and agri-tech, I've noticed something interesting about top performers. They weren't necessarily working longer hours than everyone else; they were simply more attuned to opportunities in everyday situations. The line between their personal and professional lives wasn't erased, it was just more ... permeable.

The days of 'I'm only a salesperson from 9 to 5' are as outdated as floppy disks. Today's sales champions understand that opportunities don't follow office hours. They don't need a desk, a formal meeting or even a business suit to make meaningful connections. Whether you're chatting with a stranger on a flight, attending your cousin's wedding or just scrolling through LinkedIn while waiting for your coffee order, you're surrounded by potential opportunities.

So how do you develop this ever-alert, opportunity-spotting superpower without becoming that person everyone avoids at family gatherings? Let me show you.

The Always-On Mindset: Opportunity Awareness Without Being a Sales Shark

A few months ago, I took my family on a vacation to Goa. One evening, while lounging on the beach and soaking in the sunset, I struck up a casual conversation with a fellow vacationer who was reading a novel. We talked books, business and life—and I soon learnt that he was the CEO of a multinational company.

He shared that the past year had been rough for his organisation. Morale was low, and he was looking for a meaningful gift for his leadership team—something that would inspire them, speak to the power of resilience and help them bounce back with the same energy and belief he carried. He was also considering sales training to re-energise his people.

Did I immediately pitch my book right there on the beach? Absolutely not—we were both in swimwear, after all! Instead, I just listened. I asked him a few thoughtful questions, shared a couple of personal stories about tough times and turnarounds and left it at that.

Two weeks later, he got in touch. Not only did he order copies of my book for his entire leadership team but he also became a good friend.

The real win wasn't that I made a sale. It was that I didn't even try to sell. I just showed up as a fellow human being with something valuable to share. That's the secret sauce: offer value first, the sale will follow.

When you operate with a 24x7 mindset, you're not constantly selling; you're constantly adding value. You're looking for ways to be helpful, to solve problems, to make meaningful connections. The sales work takes care of itself naturally.

A travel agent from Delhi, Sunil Verma, embodies this approach. Even when he's 'off duty' at family gatherings or social events, Sunil listens attentively for mentions of travel plans. If someone brings up plans for an upcoming trip, he doesn't launch into a commission-hungry sales pitch. Instead, he shares useful information about destinations, offers to WhatsApp some beautiful e-brochures or mentions deals that might save them money.

The key difference? He's proactive, not pushy. He offers value to those who express genuine interest, creating win-win situations rather than awkward hard-sells.

'But, Rohit,' you might be thinking, 'doesn't this mean I'm basically working all the time?' Not at all! It means you're present, observant and ready to help when opportunities naturally arise. Think of it as Alexa or Siri who are always listening for you to call out their names.

To develop this natural awareness:

- *Sharpen your observation skills:* People constantly signal their needs and interests in conversation. Train yourself to notice these hints.
- *Ask better questions:* Instead of 'What do you do?', try 'What's keeping you busy these days?' The answers will reveal far more about potential needs.
- *Listen for pain points:* When someone mentions a challenge or frustration, that's your cue to think about how you can help.
- *Position yourself as a resource:* Offer value first—an article, an introduction, a quick tip—before ever mentioning your product.

I've found that the most successful 24x7 salespeople aren't those who talk about their products all the time. They're the ones who've trained themselves to spot needs others miss, and to connect those needs to solutions in a way that feels helpful, not sales.

Networking: Your 24x7 Sales Multiplier

When I was transforming sales teams at the agri-products company, I noticed an interesting pattern: our top performers spent about 20 per cent of their time on 'non-selling' activities like attending industry events, participating in online forums and being active in professional groups.

These activities weren't directly generating sales, yet these salespeople consistently outperformed their colleagues who focused exclusively on direct selling activities. Why? Because they understood the power of networking.

The maths is simple but powerful: the wider your network, the greater your chances of connecting with potential clients. Every new person in your network isn't just one potential customer; they're a gateway to their entire network.

Take Pratham, a real estate agent in Gurgaon. While his colleagues were cold-calling from office directories, Pratham was attending real estate seminars, joining community groups and participating in city development forums. He didn't just collect business cards like Pokémon cards; he followed up consistently, offering valuable market insights and building genuine connections.

Within eighteen months, Pratham was outselling his nearest competitor by 300 per cent. His secret weapon? A vast, engaged network that generated a steady stream of warm referrals.

The PREPARE framework

To build your own powerful network, keep my PREPARE framework in mind:

- *Proactive:* Don't wait for opportunities; create them by attending events and joining communities where your potential customers gather.

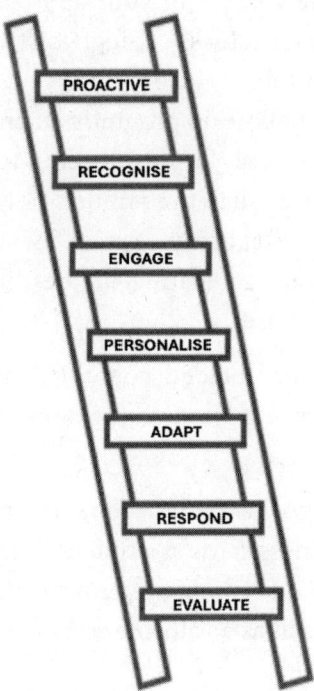

- *Recognise:* Train yourself to identify potential prospects in everyday interactions by listening for needs that align with your solutions.
- *Engage:* Start meaningful conversations by asking questions about their challenges rather than talking about your products.
- *Personalise:* Remember details about the people you meet and reference them in follow-ups to create more meaningful connections.

- *Adapt:* Be flexible in your approach—what works in a formal business setting won't work at a friend's dinner party.
- *Respond:* Follow up promptly when someone shows interest—ideally within twenty-four hours while you're still fresh in their mind.
- *Evaluate:* Regularly assess which networking activities are generating the best leads and double down on those.

This framework has helped countless sales professionals transform networking from an awkward obligation into a powerful sales driver.

Remember: the goal isn't to become the person frantically handing out business cards at a funeral (please don't be that person!). It's about becoming genuinely interested in others, positioning yourself as a valuable resource and staying alert to opportunities.

Everyday Opportunities: Turning Regular Life into a Sales Canvas

When I conduct sales leadership workshops across India, I often ask participants: 'Where was the most unusual place you ever closed a sale?' The answers never cease to amaze me:

- 'In a hospital waiting room while my wife was in labour.'
- 'During a cricket match when the person next to me mentioned needing exactly what I sell.'
- 'While getting a haircut—my barber became a client!'

These stories highlight a fundamental truth: opportunities don't confine themselves to office hours or formal settings. Your entire life is a canvas for potential sales—if you have the right mindset.

Let me walk you through some everyday scenarios that can become fertile ground for sales opportunities.

Social Events: The Natural Networking Gold Mine

Weddings, birthdays and dinner parties create a relaxed atmosphere that's perfect for organic conversations. At my niece's wedding last year, I met someone who mentioned struggling with employee training. As the founder of Laugh Every Day—Nirvana (my laughter yoga initiative), I shared how laughter-based team-building exercises had helped similar organisations. I didn't push for a sale because few people want to talk shop at a such functions; I simply offered value in the conversation. Three weeks later, he called to book a corporate workshop.

So, listen for problems you can solve, share brief insights when relevant and exchange contacts only if there's genuine interest. Remember that you're a guest first, salesperson second.

Personal Milestones: Celebrations with Opportunities

Housewarmings, job promotions and anniversaries often signal new needs or life changes. My cousin Udit, a smart wealth consultant, attended a housewarming party, and during the conversations discovered how misinformed people are about the work he does. He casually mentioned how modern wealth managers could take care of their money better by developing the right financial portfolio. By focusing on their specific needs and answering questions naturally, he converted two attendees into customers.

Always look for needs related to the milestone, offer congratulations first and solutions second and consider bringing a small, relevant gift—maybe a book on personal finance, a money plant or simply a diary with personal finance tips—that showcases your product's value.

Festivals: Seasonal Selling Opportunities

Festivals like Diwali, Holi or Christmas create natural opportunities to introduce products or services that enhance celebrations. When I was at Maruti Suzuki, we created special 'Diwali Family Package' offers that our sales team could casually mention at festival gatherings. The key was framing these as helpful information rather than pushy sales tactics. Create season-specific bundles or offers, emphasise how your product enhances the celebration and use the festive mood to build goodwill that extends beyond the season.

Educational Institutions: Targeted Audience Connections

Schools, colleges and training centres gather precisely defined audiences with specific needs. When I launched my book, I connected with business schools to offer guest lectures on corporate leadership. This positioned me as an expert while introducing my book to the exact audience who would benefit most.

Volunteer as a guest speaker, sponsor relevant events or competitions and focus on providing educational value that subtly showcases your expertise.

Travel Scenarios: Captive Audience Conversations

Flights, train journeys, hotel lobbies and even ride-shares create unique opportunities for meaningful conversations. I once sat next to a manufacturing executive on a flight from Delhi to Mumbai. After chatting about industry challenges, I shared how my leadership training had helped similar companies. That 'chance' meeting turned into a year-long consulting engagement.

Start with genuine small talk, listen for professional details that might signal needs and exchange contacts only when there's mutual interest in continuing the conversation.

The beauty of these everyday scenarios is their natural, low-pressure environment. People are more receptive when they don't feel 'sold to'. By approaching these situations with genuine interest in others and a mindset of service rather than selling, you transform ordinary moments into extraordinary opportunities.

Remember: the goal isn't to turn every social interaction into a sales pitch—that's the fastest way to lose friends and influence no one. You should be able to recognise genuine opportunities where your offering solves a real need, and approach those moments with authenticity and value.

Social Media: Your 24x7 Sales Representative

I regularly leverage social media to create opportunities while I sleep, eat or spend time with family. It's not a side hustle for me; it's a powerful extension of my 24x7 sales mindset.

I think of JhaJi Store often when I'm working with social media. The home-made pickle brand from rural Bihar appeared on Shark Tank India a few years ago. Through strategic social media marketing, they grew from a small family operation to generating a ₹60-lakh monthly revenue—all without a traditional sales force or brick-and-mortar stores. Their products sell while they sleep because they've mastered the art of passive selling through digital channels. That's the inspiration we all need.

Building Your Own 24x7 Digital Sales Presence

Here's how you can build your own 24x7 digital sales presence:

Schedule Content During Peak Engagement Times

Tools like CanvaPro and Hootsuite allow you to create and schedule posts to go live when your audience is most active—even if you're busy with other activities. I use this approach with my LinkedIn content, scheduling posts about sales leadership and team development during high-engagement morning hours when I'm often conducting workshops. Analyse your audience's online behaviour and schedule content for their prime browsing times—not when it's convenient for you to post.

Cross-Platform Leverage

Different platforms reach different segments of your audience. I repurpose my content across LinkedIn (for professional insights), Instagram (for visual workshop highlights) and Twitter (for quick sales tips). This maximises reach without multiplying effort. Create a core piece of content, then adapt it to fit each platform's unique format and audience expectations.

Direct Messaging for Personalised Engagement

When someone comments on my posts or shows interest in my services, I respond promptly—even if I'm at a family dinner or watching a cricket match. These quick, personalised interactions often lead to sales conversations that would never happen through broadcast content alone. Set up notifications and develop quick response templates that you can personalise in seconds.

Automated Ad Campaigns That Work While You Don't

Targeted advertising on platforms like Facebook, Instagram and LinkedIn can reach specific audience segments based on demographics, interests and behaviours. I've helped sales teams set up campaigns that generate qualified leads around the clock. Create ads that address specific pain points, use detailed targeting to reach the right audience and set up automated lead capture systems.

Community Engagement Beyond Your Own Profiles

Some of my best clients have come from participating in industry forums, LinkedIn groups and specialised online communities. By answering questions and providing value in spaces where your expertise is relevant, you position yourself as a trusted resource rather than just another salesperson. Identify three to five key online communities where your potential clients gather, and participate regularly without immediate trying to sell your product.

The beauty of social media is that it extends your reach exponentially while allowing you to maintain the same value-first approach that works in face-to-face situations. You don't need to be a digital salesperson who spams everyone's feeds; just position yourself as a helpful resource that's available whenever required.

Balancing the 24x7 Mindset: Staying Alert Without Burning Out

Now, I can almost hear you thinking: 'Rohit, this sounds exhausting! Am I never allowed to relax?'

As I said earlier in the chapter, developing a 24x7 sales mindset doesn't mean sacrificing your personal life or working yourself to burnout. In fact, it should make your work more integrated and enjoyable, not more overwhelming. Here's how to maintain that crucial balance:

Set Healthy Boundaries

Even with an always-on mindset, you need dedicated time away from work mode. For me, family dinners and Sunday mornings are sacred—no business calls, no checking emails. These boundaries actually make me more effective when

I'm working. Define specific times or situations where you're fully 'off-duty', and honour those boundaries rigorously.

Practise Mindful Presence

The 24x7 mindset isn't about being distracted by sales opportunities during personal moments; it's about being fully present wherever you are, which actually makes you more likely to notice genuine opportunities when they arise naturally. When you're with family or friends, be fully there. The awareness of potential opportunities should be processing in the background and not be your primary focus.

Create Systems That Work for You

Use technology to minimise the administrative aspects of your 24x7 approach. Set up automated follow-up sequences, use CRM apps to quickly log new contacts and create templates for common responses. I use voice-to-text to capture contact details and conversation notes immediately after meeting someone interesting, which takes just seconds.

Focus on High-Value Activities

Not all 24x7 opportunities are created equal. Learn to recognise which situations and connections have the highest potential value, and focus your energy there rather than trying to turn every interaction into a sales opportunity. Apply the 80/20 rule—80 per cent of your results will come from 20 per cent of your activities. Identify that crucial 20 per cent and prioritise accordingly.

The 24x7 mindset, when properly applied, should feel liberating rather than constraining. It's about removing artificial boundaries between 'work' and 'life' so that opportunities can flow naturally in both directions. Bring your authentic, helpful self to every interaction instead of compartmentalising your professional identity.

In my own journey from corporate leadership roles to author and consultant, the most valuable opportunities have often come from unexpected places and unplanned interactions, some of which I have mentioned earlier in the book. By maintaining an aware, value-first approach in all areas of life, I've discovered connections and possibilities I would have missed entirely if I had maintained a rigid nine-to-five sales mentality.

Final Thoughts: The Everyday Salesperson

Early in my career, I thought sales was all about sharp scripts, relentless follow-ups and outworking everyone in the room.

How wrong I was! Sustainable success doesn't come from hustle alone but from *awareness*. From treating every interaction, formal or informal, as part of the sales conversation.

I learnt that the most effective salespeople don't just *do* sales; they *live* it. They listen better at dinner tables, ask sharper questions at networking events and notice things others miss in everyday conversations.

Good salespersons don't have a switch they flip on in meetings; they have a 24x7 mindset they carry everywhere.

They aren't looking to turn every moment into a transaction, but recognise that opportunities don't follow a schedule. They've integrated it so naturally into their way of being that *opportunities find them as much as they find opportunities.* By staying alert, offering value and being prepared to engage meaningfully whenever opportunities arise, they transform from someone who 'does sales' into someone who embodies the essence of helpful connection.

As you develop this mindset, you'll find that sales becomes less of a dedicated activity and more of an integrated approach to life. Your radar for needs and opportunities will strengthen naturally. Your ability to connect meaningfully with others will deepen. And, yes, your sales numbers will grow—often in ways you never could have planned or predicted.

So, as you go about your day—whether you're in a formal business meeting or a casual social gathering—remember that the seeds of your next great sale could be waiting in the most unexpected places. Stay curious, lead with value and watch as the world becomes your sales canvas.

Rohit's Summary Snapshot

- *Opportunity awareness is a superpower:* Train yourself to recognise potential needs in everyday conversations without coming across as sales-obsessed.
- *Value first, sale second:* In every interaction, focus on being helpful and solving problems rather than pushing for immediate sales.

- *Your network is your net worth:* Strategically expand your connections through the PREPARE framework, focusing on quality relationships rather than trying to know everyone.
- *Every environment is a potential sales canvas:* From social events to travel scenarios, opportunities exist everywhere when you approach them with authenticity.
- *Leverage digital tools for 24x7 presence:* Use social media and automation to extend your reach and generate opportunities even when you're not actively working.
- *Balance is essential:* Maintain clear boundaries and practise mindful presence to prevent burnout while keeping your opportunity radar active.
- *Integration beats compartmentalisation:* The most natural and effective approach is to weave your sales awareness into your authentic self rather than switching between 'work mode' and 'personal mode'.

In Conclusion: A Tale That Made Me Chuckle

Let me leave you with a story that still makes me chuckle while perfectly illustrating the 24x7 mindset. It was narrated to me by a school friend who insists that he wasn't inebriated when it happened.

A few years ago, this friend attended a lavish Delhi wedding with his wife. During the reception, he noticed a sharply dressed gentleman who seemed to be having animated conversations with various guests. He didn't seem part of either family, yet he moved through the crowd with remarkable confidence.

Curious, my friend eventually found himself next to him at the buffet. 'Great spread, isn't it?' he said, making conversation.

'Absolutely! Delhi weddings are the best for networking,' he replied cheerfully.

Something about his choice of words caught my friend's attention. 'Are you a friend of the bride or groom?' he asked.

The man laughed and lowered his voice. 'Neither! I work in luxury real estate. I've found that high-end weddings are filled with exactly my target audience, so I attend one or two every weekend during wedding season.'

My friend was stunned. 'You're gatecrashing weddings to find clients?'

'I prefer to call it "optimising social opportunities",' he grinned. 'I dress well, bring generous gifts and only talk business if people ask what I do. I've closed more deals here than in my office all month!'

Before my friend could respond, an older gentleman approached and greeted the man warmly. 'Subhash! The unit you showed us in Gurgaon is perfect. We're ready to move forward!'

Excusing himself with a wink, the gatecrasher handed my friend his card and whispered, 'Twenty-four seven, my friend. Opportunities are everywhere if you're brave enough to show up.'

Now, am I suggesting you start gatecrashing weddings too? Absolutely not! That's taking the 24x7 mindset several steps too far (and might get you thrown out by security).

But there's a valuable lesson here: opportunities rarely present themselves when and where you expect them. Sales professionals who restrict themselves to conventional settings and traditional hours will always be outperformed by those who recognise that in today's connected world, every interaction is a potential gateway to opportunity.

Just make sure you're actually invited to the wedding first.

STEP 10: INVEST IN YOU

If there's one thing this version of Anand Prakash has learnt from decades in the automobile industry, it's that sales success isn't built merely on a script, a product or a pitch. It's built on *you*.

Your skills, mindset and energy shape every interaction and determine the outcome of every deal. Since you—the sales professional—are the most important factor of any deal, how do you take care of yourself?

Think of a high-performance Ferrari. No matter how sleek the design or powerful the engine, without regular servicing, it can't perform at its best. Sales is no different. Without constant self-investment, you'll burn out, lose relevance or fail to connect with today's customers.

Success in this field requires constantly upgrading yourself and your skill set. And investing in yourself doesn't mean spending fortunes or working around the clock. It about making smart, intentional decisions to sharpen your skills, build confidence and stay ahead of the competition. This chapter is your roadmap to personal and professional transformation—and it starts today.

Why Self-Investment Matters

Let's start with the basics of why does self-investment matter so much in sales.

- *Sales is about trust:* Customers don't just buy products; they buy into you. A confident, knowledgeable salesperson inspires trust, making customers feel like they're in good hands.
- *The cost of stagnation:* Failing to grow means falling behind. Markets change, customer preferences evolve and new competitors enter the scene. I've seen talented salespeople become obsolete simply because they refused to adapt to digital tools or changing buyer behaviours.
- *The long-term payoff:* Every skill you develop, every improvement you make pays dividends for years. Better pitches lead to better results, which result in promotions, opportunities and financial growth. I've watched junior sales associates transform into top performers simply by investing in themselves consistently.

A salesperson has to be prepared. And preparation begins with you and a 'growth mindset'.

The Growth Mindset for Sales

If there's one thing that separates top performers from the rest, it's their mindset. High achievers aren't just talented; they're relentless learners. They don't see challenges as roadblocks but as opportunities to grow.

A growth mindset is the belief that you can improve with effort. Instead of fearing failure, embrace it as part of the process. When a deal falls through, ask yourself: what can I learn from this? Did I miss a customer cue? Was my pitch too aggressive? Reflect, adjust and try again.

I remember Suresh, a salesperson at Sajni Lehengas in Delhi's Sarojini Nagar Market. Suresh would often supply clothes to my wife's family. He relied heavily on traditional sales strategies for years. However, when the pandemic struck, foot traffic plummeted and sales dropped significantly. That's when someone suggested he explore digital marketing.

Taking the advice seriously, Suresh began learning about social media platforms and started posting regularly about the latest offers, complete with pictures of newly arrived lehengas. His efforts paid off. By leveraging online selling, he not only revived his business but also turned a struggling business profitable. All it took was his willingness to embrace something new and adapt to changing times.

Suresh's example shows us that success isn't about one big breakthrough; it's about daily habits. I recommend scheduling time each day for reflection, goal-setting and practice. Remember: small, consistent efforts multiply over time—just like compound interest on your investments.

Key Strategies for Personal Growth

Now that you know why the mindset matters, let's talk about actionable strategies to grow.

Continuously Learn

Sales is a dynamic field. What worked last year may not do so today. That's why staying updated is critical.

Use online resources abundantly. Platforms like LinkedIn Learning, YouTube or Coursera offer courses tailored to sales professionals. Webinars and podcasts are excellent for bite-sized learning—I often listen to them during my morning commute. Stay curious. Read industry newsletters, attend product launches and ask questions to those in the know. Knowledge is power, and in sales it directly translates to revenue.

I'll give you an example. One of my children's college friends, Shipra, is a salesperson at a FabIndia store in Noida. She noticed that many customers were increasingly asking about sustainable and eco-friendly clothing options.

Recognising this as a growing trend, she subscribed to newsletters like *Business of Fashion* and followed sustainability-focused fashion influencers on Instagram. Armed with insights about materials like organic cotton and processes like natural dyeing, Shipra began suggesting specific products to environmentally conscious shoppers. Within three months, her average sales per customer increased by 15 per cent, and her manager noticed a sharp rise in customer feedback praising her expertise.

Master Core Skills

Mastering core skills like communication, negotiation and objection handling is the cornerstone of sales success, and these aren't skills you learn once—they require constant refinement.

Start by practising active listening. I've found that most customers will tell you exactly what they need if you just shut up and listen! Improve your pitch and hone non-verbal cues to connect with customers more effectively.

Use role-play sessions with colleagues to rehearse negotiation techniques, such as anchoring strong proposals and addressing objections. Create your own objection bank with prepared responses to common pushbacks. Incorporate storytelling into your pitch to connect emotionally with customers. I've closed many deals in my career by sharing relatable stories.

Polish Your Appearance and Presence

First impressions always matter, and as a salesperson your appearance speaks volumes before you even say a word. A well-groomed, confident salesperson radiates professionalism and trust, setting the stage for a successful interaction.

Ensure your clothes are neatly ironed and appropriate for your audience—smart casual for some industries, formal for others—and pay attention to details like polished shoes and accessories that are clean and understated.

Maintain proper hygiene. Fresh breath, a pleasant scent, a neat hairstyle and short, clean nails signal attentiveness. For those dealing with long hours or outdoor work, carry essentials like a comb, deodorant and a handkerchief for quick touch-ups. There is no greater turnoff than bad odour or a sticky handshake—I've experienced both from other salespeople, and I couldn't get away fast enough!

Beyond grooming, your posture and body language are just as critical: stand tall, make eye contact and smile warmly to exude confidence and approachability. Your posture, gestures and eye contact can make or break trust in face-to-face meetings. Practise confident and open body language to reinforce your message.

Leverage Training

Investing in training is one of the fastest and most effective ways to upskill in sales. Structured workshops, webinars and certifications can refine your techniques, broaden your knowledge base and boost your confidence.

Platforms like Udemy and Coursera provide flexible, self-paced courses, while live workshops from companies like the National Institute of Information Technology (NIIT) offer immersive, hands-on learning.

Dwarkesh, a salesperson in Chhattisgarh, used his two-hour daily commute to complete certifications in presentation techniques and sales strategies via Think School. In just three months, his closing rates improved significantly, and he started receiving praise from clients for his engaging pitches.

Similarly, Priya, a real estate agent in Mumbai, attended a weekend workshop on digital marketing organised by the Federation of Indian Chambers of Commerce and Industry

(FICCI), where she learnt to leverage social media for lead generation. Within weeks, she was attracting higher-quality leads and engaging more effectively with prospects online.

Sales professionals in India can also explore government-supported platforms like the Skill India initiative or micro, small, and medium enterprises (MSMEs) workshops that often provide region-specific training in customer management, negotiation and tech tools. Frankly, your best starting point is Google or ChatGPT.

Find the Right Mentor

Finding the right mentor is like securing a personal coach for your career, someone who provides insights, guidance and practical advice you can't get from books or courses.

A great mentor is experienced, approachable and skilled in the specific areas where you want to grow, whether it's mastering negotiation, refining your pitch or understanding customer psychology.

Start by observing potential mentors within your organisation or network—notice how they handle objections, close deals or navigate difficult customers. I found my first mentor by simply watching how a senior salesperson handled a particularly difficult customer with ease and grace.

Approach them respectfully, explaining what you hope to learn and why you admire their expertise. Once you connect, shadow them during sales meetings or customer interactions to see their strategies in action. Meet them regularly to discuss your progress, ask questions and recalibrate your goals based on their feedback.

I've been on both sides of mentorship, and it's equally rewarding to be the mentor as it is to be the mentee. The lessons flow both ways.

Undertake Mystery Shopping for Insights

Observing your competitors can teach you what to replicate and what to avoid. Conducting mystery shopping allows you to gain valuable insights first-hand.

Visit competitor stores or websites posing as a customer, and carefully observe their product offerings, pricing strategies and sales approaches. Engage with their sales staff to understand how they handle objections, highlight product features or create urgency. Use these observations to refine your pitches and improve your offerings.

I regularly send team members to experience our competitors' showrooms. The insights they bring back—from how Mercedes-Benz handles test drives to the way Audi presents its finance options—have been game changers for our approach.

Network with a Purpose

A strong network is a treasure trove of knowledge, mentorship and opportunities. Be proactive in building connections and nurture relationships that align with your growth goals.

Attend industry events, and join networking forums, trade expos and seminars in your field. For example, FICCI, Assocham or Confederation of Indian Industry (CII) often host sales-specific meetups in India. Networking groups like Entrepreneurs' Organization (EO), Young Presidents' Organization (YPO), Business Networking International (BNI), etc., can substantially boost your career in the long term.

Platforms like LinkedIn are perfect for engaging with sales thought leaders and participating in real-time discussions. I've found some of my best hires and business opportunities through consistent LinkedIn networking.

Build Your Tech Backbone

Leverage technology to supercharge your growth by incorporating modern tools and platforms that make self-improvement seamless and efficient.

Apps like Thinkific and Skillshare offer tailored courses to enhance soft skills and sales techniques, while AI tools like Gong.io or Chorus.ai analyse recorded sales calls to provide insights on tone, pacing and effective language that you can then work on.

Use content aggregators like Flipboard to stay updated with industry news, market trends and competitor activities in one easy-to-read format. YouTube, with its tutorials on content creation, platform algorithms and audience engagement, is another invaluable resource for mastering social media strategies.

Additionally, mastering CRM tools like HubSpot or Zoho CRM can streamline your sales process, improve customer tracking and ensure that you stay organised and responsive in every interaction.

Build Your Personal Brand

In the digital age, your online presence is as crucial as your in-person skills, making personal branding and social media mastery essential for sales success.

Start by optimising your LinkedIn profile to showcase your achievements, skills and testimonials, positioning yourself as a thought leader by regularly sharing industry-specific content.

Create engaging posts, such as tips or success stories, to attract attention from peers, mentors and potential customers. Actively participate in LinkedIn groups, industry forums or Twitter chats to expand your network and build meaningful connections.

I've personally seen how building my brand on LinkedIn has opened doors to speaking engagements, business partnerships and even my consulting practice. Your digital footprint can work for you 24x7—invest in it wisely.

Volunteer for Stretch Assignments

Stretch assignments are a powerful way to accelerate growth, build new skills and showcase initiative.

Take on roles outside your comfort zone—like leading team presentations, managing product launches or organising customer engagement events—to sharpen your leadership and project management abilities. Mentoring juniors can also boost your expertise along with supporting their development.

For instance, I knew a senior sales associate—Rajesh—who worked at Britannia Industries. He volunteered to assist the marketing team during the launch of a premium biscuit range.

By reviewing sales data, he identified an untapped opportunity in corporate gifting—a segment that valued premium packaging and brand perception. Rajesh's suggestion to create tailored gift packs for this audience drove significant orders during the holiday season, boosting revenue and earning him recognition for innovation and collaboration.

Enhance Your EQ

Developing emotional intelligence is a game changer in sales. It enables you to build stronger relationships, understand unspoken needs and handle objections with grace.

Pay attention to non-verbal cues, such as tone or body language, which can reveal customer concerns or preferences. For instance, Sneha, a pharmaceutical sales representative, noticed a doctor hesitating during her pitch about a new medication.

Instead of pushing ahead, she paused and asked, 'Is there something specific you're worried about?' This prompted a discussion about dosage safety, which she addressed with data, securing the doctor's confidence—and a significant order.

I would also recommend using stress management techniques, such as deep breathing or mindfulness apps like

Headspace or Calm, to stay composed during high-pressure situations. I practice five minutes of mindfulness before important client meetings, and it's remarkable how much clearer and more present I feel.

By honing your EQ, you can turn every interaction into a meaningful connection, enhancing loyalty and boosting sales outcomes. In luxury sales especially, I've found that EQ often makes the difference between a one-time transaction and a lifelong client relationship. This is because customers are not just buying a watch or a car—they're buying what it says about them. That's why emotional cues, subtle empathy and deep listening become critical.

Read Beyond Sales

Standing out is always better than fitting in, especially in the sales field. That's how a customer will remember you. Go that extra mile and expand your knowledge with books that teach more than traditional techniques and focus on practical strategies for negotiation and personal growth.

Start with classics like *How to Win Friends and Influence People* by Dale Carnegie, a timeless guide to building rapport and trust with people, or *The Greatest Salesman in the World* by Og Mandino, which offers motivational lessons through an engaging story.

For practical negotiation advice, try *You Can Negotiate Anything* by Herb Cohen, which simplifies complex concepts. If you're looking to build better habits, *The 7 Habits of Highly Effective People* by Stephen Covey provides actionable steps for personal and professional success.

For sales-focused inspiration, Jeffrey Gitomer's *The Little Red Book of Selling* delivers quick, easy-to-apply ideas to close more deals.

Other interesting books in this space are: *To Sell is Human* by Daniel H. Pink, *The Psychology of Selling* by Brian Tracy, *Secrets of Closing the Sale* by Zig Ziglar, *SPIN Selling* by Neil Rackham, *What Great Salespeople Do* by Michael Bosworth and Ben Zoldan and *The Science of Selling* by David Hoffeld.

These accessible reads will give you the skills and confidence needed to excel, even if you're new to self-improvement through reading. Just remember to actually practise the tips they share.

Personal Development Plan Using GROW

I started this chapter by emphasising a growth mindset. You can create a systematic plan for tracking personal development through the adoption of a GROW framework.

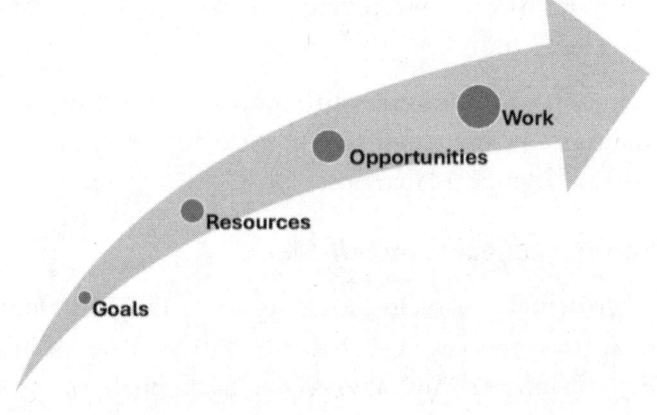

- *Goals:* Set clear and achievable goals for your development. For example, you can set a goal of achieving a 10 per cent increase in sales within the next four weeks.
- *Resources:* Identify the resources needed to achieve your goals—the tools, techniques, mentors, network—find them and start your journey.
- *Opportunities:* Continuously seek opportunities for learning and growth like workshops or seminars on advanced sales techniques.
- *Work:* Put in the effort and practise your skills regularly. There is simply no substitute for consistent hard work.

A structured GROW approach helps you set and achieve personal development goals. Work with a five-year vision for your career. Break it into actionable steps and track your progress.

Along the way, recognise milestones—completing a course, mastering a skill or improving your closing rate. Celebration fuels motivation.

I've used this framework with hundreds of sales professionals, and those who commit to it consistently outperform their peers by significant margins.

Sales Champions Are Self-Made

After decades of seeing what separates the stars from the strugglers in sales, I've become a true believer in self-investment. It's not always the slick pitch or product knowledge that ultimately drives success; it's who you are and how deliberately you've developed yourself.

Early in my career, I had a colleague named Vinod who was known for his silver tongue. The man could talk zebra stripes onto a horse! But despite his natural charm, his numbers always plateaued after the initial success. Meanwhile, another colleague, Siddhesh, who was painfully shy when he started, consistently outperformed everyone after his first year.

What was the difference? While Vinod relied solely on his natural talent, Siddhesh invested in himself relentlessly. He recorded his sales calls and analysed them every evening. He attended every optional training session. He even convinced a top performer from another branch to mentor him over weekends.

One day, I asked Siddhesh about his transformation from newbie to top performer. He laughed and said, 'Anand, anyone can look good driving a Mercedes on a straight road with perfect conditions. It's how you handle the unexpected curves that separates the amateurs from the professionals.'

That wisdom has stayed with me for decades. Siddhesh showed me that sales champions aren't born; they're self-made. They treat themselves like high-performance machines that need regular maintenance, upgrades and fine-tuning. They read voraciously, seek mentors, embrace technology and never stop refining their approach. Be that person.

Some Stuff to Revisit

- *You are the product:* Your mindset, energy and skills drive every sale. Upgrade regularly.
- *Think like a Ferrari:* Without regular tuning, even the best burn out. Keep learning.
- *Sharpen your edge:* Master core skills—pitching, listening, negotiating—through constant practice.
- *Dress the part:* First impressions matter. Look sharp and act confident.
- *Train smart:* Tap into online courses, workshops and government programmes to stay ahead.
- *Find mentors*: Learn from those who've been there. Growth accelerates with guidance.
- *Spy and learn:* Visit competitors, and notice what works and what doesn't.
- *Network with intent:* Connect where it counts—events, forums, LinkedIn.
- *Tech up:* Use tools, CRMs and AI to boost your efficiency and insight.
- *Build your brand:* Be known for your value—online and offline.
- *Stretch yourself:* Say yes to new roles. Growth lives outside your comfort zone.
- *Boost your EQ:* Read the room, stay calm and connect emotionally.
- *Read wide, think big:* Yes, read sales books, but develop as a whole person.

- *Use GROW:* Set goals, find resources, seek opportunities and put in the work.
- *Winners aren't born—they're made:* Invest in youself, and watch the ROI explode.

STEP 11: LEVERAGE THE CRISIS

Crisis—it's a word that makes even the most seasoned sales professionals break into a cold sweat. In my long career, I've seen it all: furious customers storming in over delivery delays, product malfunctions that couldn't have happened at worse times and miscommunication that spiralled into social media nightmares.

But here's what I, Rohit Goel, have learnt: it's not the crisis that defines you; *it's how you respond to it that truly matters.*

A customer once brought his brand-new car back to one of our showrooms. He was absolutely livid because the engine light came on during an important road trip with his family. Was it a disaster? Initially, yes. But by the time he left—with a loaner car, a technician personally assigned to fix his vehicle overnight and a complimentary detailing service—he'd become one of our most loyal advocates.

That's the secret of crisis management: every crisis is an unscheduled opportunity to showcase your best attributes. The way you handle these moments can transform an unhappy customer into your biggest fan.

The CARE Strategy for Crisis Management

Over the years, I've developed the CARE strategy—a structured approach to handling crises that has saved countless sales relationships:

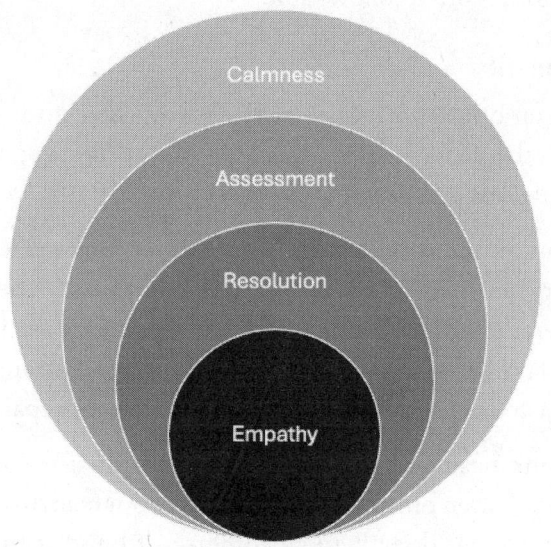

Calmness

First, calm yourself. When a customer is upset, your first instinct might be to get defensive or jump to solutions. Don't. Take a deep breath.

Let the customer vent completely without interruption. As regional head at Maruti Suzuki, I trained every sales team member to maintain eye contact, nod and genuinely listen until the customer has said everything they need to.

Phrases I've found effective include: 'I understand how frustrating this must be, and I'm here to help' or 'I can see why this situation is upsetting, and I want to make it right for you.'

Your calmness is your superpower when everything else feels chaotic. It's contagious—when you remain composed, the customer often follows suit.

Assessment

Once emotions have settled, investigate thoroughly. Get all the facts—dates, specifics of the issue, previous conversations and exactly what went wrong.

I remember a customer who claimed her new vehicle had a major transmission problem. After careful assessment, we discovered the issue was actually a driving mode setting she wasn't familiar with. Had we rushed to conclusions, we'd have wasted time and resources on unnecessary repairs.

And don't hesitate to involve relevant teams if the issue is complex. I often brought in the experts in our team to explain technical issues directly to customers—it builds credibility and shows we're taking their concerns seriously.

Resolution

This is where the rubber meets the road. Act quickly and decisively to fix the problem. Whether it's arranging a replacement, providing technical support or coordinating with suppliers, focus on removing the inconvenience as soon as possible. As Henry Ford wisely said, 'Don't find fault; find a remedy.'

You also have to keep the customer informed at every step. When we had a parts delay affecting multiple customers at General Motors, we sent daily updates even when there wasn't new information. This transparency prevented anxiety and speculation, and assured the customer that we *were* working to resolve their issue.

The speed of your response matters almost as much as the solution itself. According to Price Waterhouse Coopers, 80 per cent of American consumers consider speed to be one of the most important elements of customer satisfaction. What it means is that a quick, adequate solution outperforms a perfect but delayed one in customer satisfaction.

Empathy

Genuine empathy transforms crisis management from a transaction into a relationship-building opportunity. Show understanding through statements like: 'I'm truly sorry for the inconvenience this has caused' or 'If I were in your position, I'd feel the same way.'

But empathy goes beyond words; it's about reading the customer's emotional state. Watch their body language, listen to their tone and adjust your approach accordingly. If they're visibly upset, acknowledge it: 'I can see this has been incredibly frustrating for you.'

One of our most effective techniques is to personalise the apology. Instead of 'We apologise for the inconvenience,' try 'I'm personally sorry about what happened, and I'm taking responsibility for fixing this for you.'

Success Stories in Crisis Management

I was at my cousin Dr Amit's clinic one afternoon, waiting for my turn in the dentist's chair, when a medical sales rep walked in—confident, courteous and unusually calm. His name was Vishal Bhatnagar.

He didn't jump into a pitch. Instead, he asked about Amit's recovery from a recent shoulder injury, shared a quick update on an upcoming medical conference and then—almost as an afterthought—mentioned a new sample he thought might be worth trying.

The whole exchange lasted barely five minutes, but there was something different about it. When Vishal left, I turned to Amit and asked, 'What's so special about this guy? You looked more like friends than a doctor and a rep.'

Amit smiled and said, 'He listens. He remembers. And he genuinely cares. He doesn't just talk about the medicine—he talks about *me*.'

That moment stuck with me.

Most salespersons believe that success comes from rehearsed pitches, hitting daily call targets and rattling off product specs. But Vishal had clearly figured out the real formula: sales is a series of meaningful moments, not just a bunch of meetings. Vishal doesn't carry just samples in his bag, he carries *trust*.

And in a crowded market, that's what sets him apart.

Every Crisis Is an Opportunity

The most successful brands understand that crises can become defining moments—of course that is only after calm has been restored. Consider these examples:

When The Ritz-Carlton overbooked during a high-demand season, rather than apologising and offering discounts (the standard response), they turned it into an experience. They relocated guests to nearby five-star hotels, provided complimentary spa treatments and chauffeured them back to dine at the Ritz-Carlton. Guests shared glowing reviews about how an inconvenience became a memorable adventure.

Delta Airlines faced a massive flight disruption in 2017. Their CEO, Ed Bastian, personally oversaw the response, issued a public apology, gave travel vouchers to affected passengers and upgraded loyal customers to elite status. This proactive approach earned them widespread appreciation.

Tesla, too, showed creativity during a crisis. When their California showroom experienced a roof leak during a Model Y launch event, the team distributed branded umbrellas and joked about 'weatherproof technology'. Their humour and quick thinking entertained customers and transformed a potential disaster into a quirky win.

Managing Supply Chain Disruptions

In the automotive industry, supply chain issues happen regularly. At some companies, customers have to wait months for specialty parts or custom orders, only to face further delays. I now know how to handle these situations effectively. The first key thing is proactive communication. The moment you learn about a delay, inform your customer. I've found that customers who receive advance notice about an issue are 70 per cent less likely to cancel their order than those surprised by last-minute delays.

Next, consider alternatives. For example, when we were faced with a six-month wait for a specific trim due to chip shortages, we offered customers temporary alternatives—like upgrading them to a higher model while they waited or providing rental cars at no cost. When delays are significant, goodwill gestures go a long way. We've offered everything from free maintenance packages to accessories or discounts on future services.

I was at the receiving end of this kind of customer service from Vrinda, a salesperson at a furniture store. How she handled the matter was a good lesson from one salesperson to another. I had ordered a custom sofa from her store, but there was a delay in delivery due to a supplier issue. Vrinda promptly informed me, waived the shipping cost and offered a small discount as a goodwill gesture. By managing expectations and showing empathy, she preserved the relationship and earned positive feedback from me. I was glad to see a fellow salesperson on the same page as me when it came to managing potential crises.

Handling Complaints Effectively

The way you handle complaints can turn critics into champions. Here's my approach. First, document everything—dates, product information, the nature of the complaint. This ensures consistency in follow-ups and prevents miscommunication.

Next, set clear expectations. Explain exactly what will happen next and when. 'Our technician will examine your vehicle within twenty-four hours, and I'll personally call you by tomorrow afternoon with a diagnosis and timeline for repairs.'

It is important to simplify the process. Make resolution as easy as possible for the customer. In the service department at auto companies I worked for, we implemented a 'one-call resolution' policy—customers shouldn't need to explain their issue to multiple people.

Finally, follow through. Once the issue is resolved, the story isn't over. A well-timed follow-up can cement a positive impression. For example: 'Is everything functioning to your satisfaction now?' or 'Thank you for your patience throughout this process.' Or 'We've added a complimentary annual maintenance check to your account.'

Building Loyalty Through Crisis Management

When handled properly, a crisis can actually strengthen customer loyalty more than if nothing had gone wrong at all. It's the service recovery paradox—customers who experience a problem that's resolved extraordinarily well often become more loyal than those who never faced a problem. The key is to go beyond basic resolution.

For example, during a recall that affected several models at Maruti Suzuki, we assigned each customer a dedicated service adviser who provided personalised updates and handled all questions. The customer always knew who to get in touch with in case they had any additional queries. Next, empower the customer. Give them choices in how they want the issue to be resolved. 'Would you prefer a replacement, a repair or store credit?' This sense of control helps transform frustration into satisfaction.

Finally, make memorable gestures. One of our customers had a major electrical issue on the day of an important business meeting. Not only did we repair the car quickly but we also arranged and paid for a luxury car service to ensure he made to the meeting on time. Years later, he still tells this story when recommending us to friends.

Digital Crisis Management

In today's digital world, a single negative review or social media complaint can quickly snowball into a PR crisis. I once had a customer post about a vehicle issue that went viral locally. Instead of ignoring it, we responded publicly with empathy—saying we understood their frustration—outlined our solution and invited the customer to a personal meeting.

The result? The customer updated their post with praise for our response, turning a potential reputation disaster into positive publicity. Research by Dimensional Research (commissioned by Zendesk) shows that 45 per cent of consumers share bad customer service experiences via social media. Meanwhile, a Sprout Social report reveals that 73 per cent of customers will stop doing business with a brand if they feel ignored on social media.

Speed is critical: McKinsey found that 40 per cent of consumers expect a response within an hour, and 79 per cent within twenty-four hours, after posting complaints online. Prompt and authentic engagement can not only defuse tension but also transform critics into brand advocates.

Always monitor review platforms and social media mentions of your brand. When you spot a complaint, respond within hours—not days. Use language that's authentic and empathetic; customers can easily distinguish between a canned response and a genuine one.

Proactive Crisis Prevention

While handling crises effectively is crucial, preventing them is even better. You can so do by setting clear expectations. During the sales process, become brutally honest about delivery timelines, maintenance requirements and potential limitations. This transparency builds trust and reduces disappointment.

Another issue is feedback loops. Create multiple channels for customer feedback—surveys, follow-up calls and suggestion boxes—to catch small issues before they became crises. Of course, work closely with service teams parallelly to address recurring issues, establishing a direct line between customer complaints and quality improvements.

Running team exercises with simulated complaints and allowing staff to practise their responses in a low-pressure environment is always a good idea. Most importantly, learn from each crisis. After every significant issue, conduct a thorough post-mortem. What went wrong? How could we have prevented it? What systems needed improvement?

The Cadbury worm crisis of 2003 is a perfect example of crisis transformation. When customers discovered worms in their chocolates, the company faced a potential death blow to their brand. Instead of merely addressing the immediate issue, Cadbury conducted a comprehensive audit of their entire supply chain and discovered that inadequate retail storage conditions were the culprit.

They implemented a 'double wrapped' packaging method and launched a campaign with actor Amitabh Bachchan to reassure consumers. This response not only solved the immediate crisis but also strengthened their brand reputation by demonstrating their commitment to quality and transparency.

Rohit's Sign-Off

I've come to believe that a sales crisis is like spicy street food: it's going to hit you eventually, and it's going to test your gut. The trick isn't in avoiding it; it's in how gracefully you survive it without losing your cool ... or your customer.

Most people treat crises like they're a fire. Panic, blame, run around waving their hands. I treat them like a spotlight. You're on stage, and all eyes are on you. It's your cue to perform.

The worst thing you can do when something goes wrong? Pretend it didn't. Customers smell denial like yesterday's socks. Own the mess. Be honest. Be human. And then—here's the magic—be unexpectedly generous. Give them something they didn't expect. Solve the problem and make them laugh while you're at it.

I've seen more loyalty being built in moments of disaster than in flawless deliveries. A perfectly executed sale is nice. But turning a screw-up into a standing ovation? That's art.

So, don't aim for perfection. Aim for bounce-back ability. If you're going to fall, fall funny. Fall forward. And for God's sake, offer them a coffee while you're at it. And I guarantee you will not fail, whatever the intensity of the fall.

Key Points to Remember

- *Crisis = opportunity:* Don't fear the mess; use it to shine. Great recovery creates legendary loyalty.
- *Use the CARE strategy:* Stay calm, assess the facts, offer swift resolution and show real empathy.
- *Speed + transparency = trust:* Fast fixes and honest updates matter more than perfect solutions.
- *Own the problem:* Don't make excuses. Take responsibility and over-deliver on the resolution.
- *Digital responses count:* Monitor online chatter. Respond fast, and with heart—not a corporate script.
- *Make it memorable:* Surprise with a goodwill gesture, humour or VIP-level service.

- *Prevent before you fix:* Set clear expectations, gather feedback and train teams with real-life scenarios.
- *Bounce back > Perfection:* Customers remember how you handle the fall, not the stumble itself.

STEP 12: BUILD YOUR PERSONAL BRAND

You know what they say about your personal brand: it's what people say about you *after you've left the room*. So, for heaven's sake, make sure it's worth talking about! My career has taught me that your personal brand is your secret weapon in the battlefield of sales.

In the Anand Prakash world, it's not just what you say, but how you make people feel. From that first warm handshake to how you handle a crisis when a customer's new car breaks down on their way to a wedding, every interaction either builds or breaks your brand.

Here's the undeniable truth about sales: people buy from people they trust. And trust doesn't come from a slick pitch or fancy product demo; it comes from *you*. Your personal brand is what sets you apart, earns client loyalty and opens doors to opportunities you didn't even know existed.

Why Bother with Personal Branding?

'But, Anand,' you might ask, 'isn't selling the product enough?' Not anymore. You're not just selling a product; you're selling trust. As Zig Ziglar brilliantly put it, 'If people like you, they'll listen to you. But if they trust you, they'll do business with you.'

I remember reading about a car salesman named James Kinnan from the US who had a special way of connecting with clients. Instead of focusing on specs and discounts, he shared his personal story: 'My dad bought his first car from this dealership,' he'd tell customers, 'and I remember sitting in that car as a kid, dreaming about driving it someday.' His authenticity and passion became his brand, and his closing rate was 30 per cent higher than his colleagues.

His example shows us that people don't just buy products; they buy the person selling them.

Look at Vinita D'Souza, a SaaS account manager I met at a conference. She became known for her personalised follow-ups—always timely and genuinely helpful. When a competitor tried to poach her biggest client by undercutting her pricing by 20 per cent, the client stayed loyal, telling her, 'I trust Vinita more than I trust their discount.' That's the power of a strong personal brand.

The Building Blocks of a Personal Brand

Your personal brand isn't built overnight, but it's not rocket science either. Here's how you can lay the foundation for a brand that makes waves:

Clarity: Define Your Brand Identity

Who are you? What do you stand for? What makes you different from every other salesperson out there? If you can't answer these questions, your prospects won't be able to either.

Here's a quick exercise I give to all new hires at my dealership: write down three adjectives that describe your personality. For me, they're 'passionate', 'straight-talking' and 'dependable'.

Now, think about how these traits translate into your sales approach. My straight-talking nature means I'll tell customers if a particular model isn't right for them, even if it means losing a sale—because I know that honesty builds long-term relationships.

Authenticity: Be Real, Not Perfect

Clients can smell inauthenticity from a mile away—just like that awful cologne some salespeople bathe in before client meetings (don't be that person!).

Building trust is a marathon, not a sprint. Think of your long-term relationships as a savings account for your reputation—every authentic interaction is a deposit.

Your brand should be a genuine reflection of who you are—not who you think people want you to be. When I meet a client, I don't hide my humble beginnings. They are part of my story and help me connect with entrepreneurs who are working their way up.

Value: Lead with What You Bring to the Table

Your brand isn't just about you; it's also about the value you deliver. How do you make your clients' lives easier, their businesses more successful or their days less stressful?

Create a personal tagline that captures this value, and customise it for different scenarios. For example: 'I help you find not just a house but a home where your life's most meaningful moments will unfold.' It's simple, clear and focuses on what matters.

Consistency: Show Up the Same Way, Every Time

A great brand is predictable—not in a boring but a dependable way. Whether a client interacts with you online, in a meeting or bumps into you at their kid's football match, your message and tone should align.

I make sure my LinkedIn profile, business cards, email signature and even my voicemail all reflect the same professional but approachable tone. Small things go a long way in building consistency.

Remember the ABCD formula for branding: Authenticity, Balance (of personal and professional), Consistency and Delivery (on your promises). Miss any one of these, and your brand becomes as wobbly as a car with misaligned wheels.

Amplifying Your Brand

Building a personal brand is one thing. Making sure the world knows about it? That's another challenge entirely. Here's how to put your brand on full display:

Dominate LinkedIn and Social Media

Think of LinkedIn as your billboard on the busiest highway in the professional world. I treat my LinkedIn profile as seriously as I treat my showroom floor—it needs to be spotless, impressive and inviting.

I regularly share insights about the automotive industry, customer service tips and behind-the-scenes glimpses of my work. Recently, I posted about how electric vehicles are changing the Indian automobile landscape. It generated more engagement than posts from competitors with much larger marketing budgets.

But remember: engage, don't just broadcast. I make sure to comment on posts, ask questions and start discussions. Social media isn't a megaphone—it's a coffee shop conversation.

Public Speaking: The Fast Track to Credibility

Whether it's a local business event, an industry webinar or a sales team huddle, public speaking is a powerful way to showcase your expertise.

I know a financial adviser, Raj Sharma, who hosts free 'vada-pav-and-learn' sessions for small business owners at a local eatery. His knack for simplifying complex financial concepts while everyone enjoys Mumbai's favourite snack has turned casual attendees into loyal clients.

I've done something similar with the 'Cars & Coffee' events at my dealership, where I discuss the latest automotive technology while prospective buyers enjoy a premium brew. There's no pressure to buy—just valuable information and relationship-building.

Be the Go-To Resource

Position yourself as the person people turn to for advice, insights or solutions. I started a simple email newsletter called *The Driver's Seat* where I share car maintenance tips, industry news and answers to common customer questions. It's not fancy, but it's consistent and useful—and it keeps me top-of-mind with past customers.

Push customers to rethink their assumptions. Teach them something new about their industry, and position yourself as a trusted adviser, not just another salesperson trying to hit quota.

Personal Branding in Action

Let me share some real examples of how effective personal branding looks in practice:

The Social Media Maven

Rahul Seth, a real estate agent, uses Instagram to post short videos of market updates, home-buying tips and even funny moments from his day. Clients love his down-to-earth vibe, and he's built a following that generates leads weekly without spending a rupee on traditional advertising.

The Relationship Builder

Swati Chaturvedi, an enterprise resource planning salesperson who once worked for me, makes it a habit to send handwritten thank-you notes to clients after closing deals. That personal touch in our digital age has earned her a 90 per cent referral rate. Ninety per cent!

The Thought Leader

Kaushik Rana, a senior account manager at a tech firm, regularly shares insights from industry conferences he attends. His clients see him as a knowledgeable partner, not just a vendor pushing products.

Avoiding Common Pitfalls

Even with the best intentions, personal branding can go off the rails. Here are mistakes I've seen (and occasionally made myself):

Trying to Be Everything to Everyone

Focus on your niche. Being specific makes you memorable.

Imagine you're at a networking event, and someone introduces themselves as an expert in 'everything sales'. No specific industry, no unique expertise, just 'everything'. Would you trust them to solve your exact problem? Not likely.

Now, compare that to someone who says, 'I specialise in helping real estate buyers find properties that match both their lifestyle and investment goals.' That's targeted and memorable.

Being Overly Salesy

Your brand is about trust and value, not a constant sales pitch.

I once hired a tech sales executive, Neel, who overwhelmed our clients by bringing every conversation back to product features and closing. Instead of building trust, he became known as 'that pushy guy'. After some coaching, he learnt to add value first, pitch second. Your social media shouldn't look like a never-ending infomercial.

Neglecting Offline Branding

A strong handshake, a genuine smile and eye contact still matter tremendously.

Your brand isn't just built online. The way you carry yourself in meetings, the follow-up emails you send and even how you dress are all part of the package. I've seen too many salespeople who are LinkedIn lions but face-to-face lambs. Consistency offline matters just as much.

Action Plan: Build Your Brand Today

Want to get started right away? Here's your three-step action plan:

- *Audit your presence:* Google yourself tonight. What comes up? Does it align with how you want to be seen? I do this quarterly—checking LinkedIn, customer reviews, tagged photos and even past articles or mentions. If I spot anything off-brand, I update my profiles or content immediately. I also take insights from online reviews and apply them offline—like adjusting how I introduce myself, rephrasing my pitch or refining my follow-up style.
- *Define your message:* Write a one-sentence statement about who you are and what you do. Use it everywhere—your email signature, social profiles and when you introduce yourself.
- *Start sharing:* Post one piece of valuable content this week on LinkedIn or another platform. It doesn't need to be perfect—just helpful.

A strong personal brand isn't built overnight. But when it's built right, it pays dividends for a lifetime. Much of this comes with the reputation you build with your existing customers.

Take Shonali, an IT solutions rep I met last year who saved a deal when a client's system crashed during an implementation. By mobilising her team to fix the issue overnight, she turned a near-disaster into a loyalty win, cementing her reputation as a reliable partner.

Building your brand isn't about pretending to be a superhero; it's about being the person your clients call when their sky is falling (even if you have to wear your pyjamas to the rescue).

Crisis moments reveal your true colours. When something goes wrong—and it will—your response becomes a part of your brand story. Do you dodge responsibility, or do you step up and solve the problem? Clients remember those who stand by them when the chips are down.

Every action you take, from replying to an email to resolving a complaint, is a brush stroke on the canvas of your brand. Make every stroke count. Your personal brand isn't just about today's deal; it's about the doors it will open for you in five, ten or twenty years. It's your legacy in the world of sales.

A Page from My Journey

After two decades of building dealerships and sales teams, I've seen first-hand how personal branding separates the sales stars from the also-rans. It's your most powerful sales tool—opening doors, earning trust and keeping you top-of-mind long after the pitch.

Last year, I got a call from a customer who bought a Maruti car from one of our dealerships ten years ago. A decade ago! He remembered how I'd personally delivered the vehicle along with the dealership executive to his home when his father was ill and couldn't come to the showroom. Now he was calling to buy cars for his entire business fleet. That's the power of a personal brand that stands the test of time.

Your reputation isn't built on grand gestures but on a thousand small moments of integrity, helpfulness and genuine care. In a world where products become increasingly similar and prices more and more transparent, *you* are your ultimate differentiator.

So, start today. Be intentional about how you present yourself. Be consistent in how you communicate. Be memorable in how you serve customers. Because in the end, people may forget what you sold them, but they'll never forget how you made them feel. Your personal brand is waiting to be built. Start laying the foundation brick by brick, and watch your sales career transform from a job into a legacy.

Your Action Summary

- *You are the brand:* People don't just buy products; they buy you. Trust, not a slick pitch, drives loyalty.
- *Define your difference:* Know what makes you uniquely you—your story, strengths and style are your superpower.
- *Be real, not perfect:* Authenticity builds credibility. Don't fake it—own your quirks and experiences.

- *Deliver real value:* Show how you solve problems and ease pain points. Make it about how you're making their life easier.
- *Consistency is credibility:* Be the same online, in person and on follow-up. Reliability earns respect.
- *Go beyond selling:* Use LinkedIn, newsletters, events and conversations to share insights, not sales pitches.
- *Start small, stay steady:* Post once a week, speak at a local event send a thank-you note to customers after the sale. The little things add up.
- *Avoid common traps:* Don't try to be everything, don't oversell and don't ignore how you show up offline.
- *Crises build character:* How you act when things go wrong becomes part of your brand story. So, make it count.
- *Your brand is your legacy:* Build it moment by moment. Be memorable, be helpful and, above all, be you.

STEP 13: EMBRACE CONTINUOUS GROWTH

Jack Welch, that legendary business guru, once said, 'Change before you have to.'

If there's one thing over twenty-five years in sales leadership at multiple companies have taught me—Rohit Goel—it's that standing still is a slow way of moving backwards. The market evolves, competitors adapt and customer expectations shift faster than a GPS rerouting in a Delhi jam during monsoon chaos.

The only way to stay ahead is to embrace growth—not as some occasional sprint when you're feeling motivated but as a lifelong marathon that you run every single day.

Sales success isn't just about hitting targets (though CFOs might disagree). It's about becoming better, sharper and more adaptable with every interaction. Let me share how a growth mindset can turn you into a resilient, resourceful and, frankly, unstoppable sales machine.

Building a Growth Mindset

A growth mindset is your compass for navigating the inevitable potholes and detours of a sales career. It's about viewing that embarrassing moment when you called a client by the wrong name as a lesson in preparation, not as evidence that you're hopeless.

Along with dreaming big, sales legends pair ambition with consistent action. Take Sara Blakely, founder of Spanx. She didn't just dream of revolutionising undergarments; she turned every rejection into fuel for innovation. Her unwavering commitment to improving her pitch and product turned her into a billionaire. I keep her story taped to my desk as a reminder.

Or look at Howard Schultz, the mastermind behind Starbucks. When Schultz first pitched his crazy idea of creating a coffeehouse experience in a country that was perfectly happy with instant coffee, investors practically laughed him out of the room. Instead of sulking or giving up, Schultz refined his approach, opened his own coffee shop and eventually acquired Starbucks, turning it into the global phenomenon we know today.

As Schultz says, 'Dream more than others think practical. Expect more than others think possible.' Every time I find myself thinking small, I remember this quote and ask myself: 'What would Schultz do?'

To build this mindset in yourself:

Focus on Learning

Treat every rejection as a lesson, not a failure. After losing a major deal at Maruti, I forced myself to ask: 'What could I have done differently?' That painful analysis helped me land three massive deals the next few months.

Adapt and Innovate

Stay curiously restless. Our teams at Maruti Suzuki started experimenting with digital showrooms years before our competitors—not because we had a crystal ball but because we constantly questioned our own methods.

Celebrate Small Wins

Break big goals into smaller milestones and reward yourself along the way. When I started at General Motors, I kept a jar of Ferrero Rochers on my desk and ate one every time I hit a micro-target. By the end of the year, I had exceeded my goals and gained a few kilos. But it was worth it!

The Five Stages of Sales Growth

I've observed that most sales professionals go through five distinct stages of growth. Understanding where you are in this journey can help you focus your development efforts more effectively:

Stage 1: The Novice

We all start here—full of theoretical knowledge but short on practical experience. At this stage, you follow scripts rigidly and might struggle with objections. I remember my first week at Birla Cement. I would clutch my product information sheets like they were sacred texts, nervously anticipating the questions I couldn't answer. At this stage, focus on mastering the fundamentals. Shadow experienced colleagues, record your calls for self-review and practise handling common objections until they become second nature. That's what I did too, and it served me well.

Stage 2: The Technician

Now you're comfortable with product knowledge and basic sales techniques. You can handle routine situations but might still struggle with complex negotiations or challenging customers. At this stage, refining your questioning techniques is critical—you'll gain sharper insight into what customers truly want. Developing deeper needs analysis skills means learning to ask open-ended questions, actively listening and identifying unspoken concerns. Why does this matter? Because deeper needs analysis allows you to align your pitch more precisely with the customer's real priorities, transforming your solution from 'nice-to-have' to 'must-have'. When you uncover not just what the customer says they want but why they want it, you build stronger trust and close more meaningful deals.

Stage 3: The Strategist

At this stage, you're no longer just making sales; you're orchestrating them. You understand customer psychology and business dynamics, allowing you to anticipate needs and objections before they arise. Now is the time to develop your own unique selling methodology and start mentoring others. Expand your business acumen beyond your immediate product line to understand broader industry trends.

Stage 4: The Trusted Adviser

This is where sales transcends transactions. Customers seek your opinion on matters beyond your product because they value your perspective. You're now solving complex business problems. Deepen your expertise in specific industries or use cases. Publish content, speak at events and build a personal brand that positions you as a thought leader in your space.

Stage 5: The Visionary

Few reach this level. Visionary salespeople don't just respond to market needs; they anticipate and shape them. They see opportunities others miss and can articulate value in transformative ways. At this stage, you should be innovating sales approaches, developing new markets and mentoring the next generation. Your growth becomes about legacy and impact.

Wherever you are in this journey, remember that moving to the next stage requires deliberate effort. Comfort is the enemy of growth. As soon as you feel you've mastered your current level, it's time to push into new territory.

Goal Setting for Continuous Growth with DREAM

Setting ambitious yet realistic goals is critical. I use an acronym that's helped me and countless sales teams I've mentored: DREAM.

Here's how it works:

Define

Make sure your goals are specific and aligned with both personal and professional aspirations. 'Sell five timeshare holidays this month' is actionable; 'Improve sales' is vague. I once had a sales executive who kept saying he wanted to 'do better this quarter'. I asked him, 'Better than what? By how much? By when?' answering those questions set him on the path that had a higher growth trajectory. Specificity creates clarity.

Realistic

Establish achievable milestones. When I decided to write my first motivational book, I didn't just set a goal of 'finish book'. I broke it down: outline one chapter every weekend, write 500 words daily, edit one section each evening. Big dreams require small steps.

Evaluate

Track your performance relentlessly. Use CRM software, a bullet journal or even a simple notepad. Every evening before leaving my office, I spend ten minutes asking: what worked today? What didn't? This ritual has saved me from repeating the same mistakes.

Action Plan

Map out clear strategies for achieving your goals. When I became the regional head at Bajaj, I identified exactly which resources I needed, which team members would handle specific tasks and which metrics would tell me if we were on track.

Motivate

Find your inspiration and keep it front and centre. As motivational speaker Les Brown says, 'Shoot for the moon. Even if you miss, you'll land among the stars.' Some days, my motivation is my family; other days, it's beating last year's numbers; occasionally, it's just proving wrong the person who said I couldn't do it.

Let me tell you about Dhanesh Shah, a junior sales rep in a mid-sized tech firm I mentored. When he started, Dhanesh was tasked with selling twenty units of software monthly—a target he thought was impossible. We sat down and applied the DREAM framework to break this into actionable weekly goals: identify fifty leads, make twenty-five calls and secure five meetings each week.

By consistently hitting these micro-goals (and tracking them obsessively on his whiteboard), Dhanesh exceeded his quota by 15 per cent in his second quarter. He earned an out-of-turn promotion to area manager with a significant salary bump. Not bad for a guy who initially thought his target was impossible!

The Four Dimensions of Sales Growth

To truly excel in sales, you need to grow in four distinct dimensions: technical, business, relationship and personal. Most salespeople focus on just one or two, which limits their potential.

Technical Mastery

This dimension covers your product knowledge, sales methodologies and technical selling skills. It's the 'how' of selling—how to present, how to handle objections, how to close. I once worked with a car salesman who could recite every specification of every model on the showroom floor. But he couldn't sell because he lacked skills in the other dimensions. Technical knowledge is necessary, but it's not enough. Take certification courses, attend product training, practise with role-plays and study sales methodologies beyond your company's standard approach. Otherwise, it will be an 'operation was successful but patient is dead' kind of situation.

Business Acumen

This dimension is about understanding the broader business context in which your product operates. How does your solution impact the customer's bottom line? What industry trends are shaping their priorities? At Bajaj, I noticed our top performers weren't necessarily those who knew the most about our bikes; they were the ones who understood how transportation decisions affected their customers. Read industry publications, follow key analysts, take business courses and learn to speak the language of finance and executive leadership.

Relationship Intelligence

This dimension covers your ability to build trust, read people, establish rapport and maintain relationships over time. It's the emotional intelligence component of sales. I remember a top-class sales executive, Priya, at Maruti Suzuki who wasn't particularly charismatic or technically brilliant, but she outsold everyone because customers absolutely trusted her judgment and felt that she genuinely cared about their needs. Practise active listening, study body language, seek feedback on your interpersonal approach and develop genuine curiosity about your customers as people.

Personal Effectiveness

This final dimension is about optimising your energy management, time management, resilience and ability to perform consistently under pressure. The most brilliant sales strategy is worthless if you're too burnt out to execute it well.

In my first year as national head of sales at Bajaj, I went into a mode of sacrificing everything—sleep, exercise, even weekends. But despite the hustle, my performance began to dip. That's when I stepped back and reset. I built a morning routine, made time for fitness and started reflecting regularly. I added structure not to slow down but to stay sharp and consistent.

Real performance doesn't come from running on empty but from working with clarity, energy and balance.

Sustainable success starts with self-leadership. The magic happens when you grow in all four dimensions simultaneously. Think of them as the wheels on your car—if one is flat, the entire vehicle performs poorly. A balanced growth approach will accelerate your career faster than focusing exclusively on traditional selling skills.

The Compound Effect of Micro-Improvements

Perhaps the most powerful concept I've embraced in my own growth journey is the compound effect of micro-improvements. Most people overestimate what they can achieve in a day and underestimate what they can achieve in a year of consistent small steps.

If you improve just 1 per cent each day, after a year you'll be thirty-seven times better—not just 365 per cent better. That's the magic of compound growth.

I keep a '1% Better' notebook where I document small improvements I'm working on each week:

- Making one more call before lunch
- Learning one new feature of our CRM system
- Reading ten pages of a business book before bed
- Arriving five minutes earlier to mentally prepare for meetings.

None of these actions is revolutionary, but together they've transformed my performance over time. The top performers I've coached all share this commitment to incremental improvement—they're not trying to reinvent themselves overnight, they're just getting slightly better each day.

When I look at the most successful people in my network—from CEOs to star salespeople—the common thread isn't talent or luck. It's their unshakeable commitment to growth. They're constantly learning, adapting and evolving.

Final Ascent: Your Growth Challenge

So, ask yourself:

- What's the next mountain I want to climb in my career?
- What new skills will help me get there?
- And how will I celebrate when I reach the summit?

Now, fast-forward a year. What will you have mastered? What milestones will you have crushed? Remember: the view from the top isn't just about achievement; it's also about recognising how far you've climbed.

Growth isn't glamorous. It takes grit, resilience and daily commitment. But it's worth every drop of effort. Every book you read, every workshop you attend, every tough conversation you have with yourself after a setback—it all adds up. It compounds into mastery.

So, take that first step now. Sign up for that course you've been hesitating on. Dust off that book. Call that mentor.

Keep climbing. There's always another peak. And when you get there, the view is bloody brilliant.

Climb Higher: Growth Lessons That Stick

- *Growth is a lifestyle, not a phase:* Standing still in sales means falling behind. Evolve or become irrelevant.
- *Adopt a growth mindset:* Every mistake, rejection

and awkward moment is a stepping stone and not a setback.
- *Know where you are in your career:* From novice to visionary, recognise your position in the five-stage growth journey—and push to go to the next level.
- *Set DREAM goals:* Define. Realistic. Evaluate. Action plan. Motivate. Ambition works best when it's structured.
- *Grow in 4D:* Technical mastery, business acumen, relationship intelligence and personal effectiveness—neglect any of these, and your performance will suffer.
- *Micro-wins matter:* Improve 1 per cent daily, and you'll be thirty-seven times better in a year. Small steps create big momentum.
- *Balance beats burnout:* Hustle smart, not just hard. Energy and clarity lead to consistent excellence.
- *Success compounds:* Books, feedback, tough calls, self-reflection—stacked over time, they build greatness.

STEP 14: DETERMINE YOUR FIT

If you've read any of my previous *13 Steps* books—on luck, wealth, marks, parenting or health—you'll recall the Ashwin Sanghi tradition: I always sneak in a bonus chapter at the end. Think of it as a literary dessert, a sweet reward for sticking with us through all thirteen steps. And since you've made it this far, you've certainly earned it!

While researching for this book, I know that my co-authors, Anand and Rohit, interviewed countless sales professionals across India. We learnt that sales is often romanticised as the art of influence—a career that thrives on energy, creativity and connection. It's arguably one of the oldest professions in the world (no, not *that* one), where success isn't just about pushing products or services but about understanding people, solving problems and building trust.

But let's be brutally honest here: the sales profession isn't for everyone. The glamour of closing big deals comes bundled with its share of challenges. For every champagne-popping celebration, there are dozens of rejections, tough targets and the constant need to evolve faster than a chameleon on a rainbow.

So, if you are looking to build a career out of college, how do you determine if sales is truly your calling? Is it in your DNA, or should you look elsewhere? In this chapter, I'll break down the qualities, skills and mindset that define successful salespeople. Think of it as your personal career compatibility test—no blood samples required, just honest self-reflection.

The Essence of Salesmanship

Sales isn't just a job; it's a dynamic interplay of art and science, much like the novels I write. Just as I weave historical facts and legends with fictional narratives in my *Bharat Collection* books, a salesperson weaves compelling stories that connect a customer's needs to a product's value.

When I was researching for some of my books, I spent hours listening to storytellers who could take their audiences to different worlds. Successful salespeople do exactly that— they transport customers to a world where their problems are solved by the product being offered. They're not just selling; they're creating possibilities for a better life.

A truly effective salesperson is also a problem-solver. Instead of pushing products like a street hawker shouting about veggies, they provide solutions, often uncovering needs that even the customers may not realise they have. In essence, the role goes beyond selling—it's about delivering value that transforms lives, businesses or at least makes someone's day a little better.

Traits of a Successful Salesperson

Through my conversations with sales leaders and my own experiences running businesses before becoming an author, I've discovered that the core qualities of thriving salespeople fall into three broad categories: personal skills, interpersonal skills and professional competencies. Let's unpack these:

Personal Skills

- *Positive mindset:* This is the cornerstone of a sales career. Rejections are as inevitable as plot twists in my thrillers, but each 'no' is simply a step closer to a 'yes'. Visualise yourself like a spring—bouncing back stronger each time someone pushes you down. As one seasoned rep told me, 'A rejection isn't the end of the conversation; it's the start of a better one.' I couldn't have written a more optimistic line myself!
- *Communication skills:* A great salesperson is both a storyteller and an empathetic listener. Much like the attention I pay to historical details in my research, you need to do the same to customer cues. Ask open-ended questions and adapt your style to suit your audience. As the saying goes, 'Speak only as much as needed; listen twice as much.' My editor would be thrilled if I followed this advice more often!
- *Honesty and integrity:* Trust is the currency of sales, just as it is between an author and reader. Being transparent builds long-term relationships and ensures repeat business. When readers trust me to deliver a well-researched story, and I repay that trust, they come back for the next book. The same principle applies in sales.
- *Continuous learning:* The best salespeople never stop upgrading their skills. Whether it's mastering a

new CRM tool, catching up on product knowledge or learning from customer feedback, staying sharp and up to date is non-negotiable. I spend months researching each novel I write; a good salesperson invests similar energy in mastering their craft.
- *Troubleshooting:* Problem-solving on the fly is essential. Customers want solutions, not excuses—much like my readers expect plot holes to be resolved by the end of the book!

Interpersonal Skills

- *Empathy:* Understanding your customer's perspective is key to building trust. When I create characters, I have to see the world through their eyes—salespeople do the same with customers.
- *Relationship building:* Sales is not a transactional business; it's based on relationships. A satisfied customer is a loyal customer—and a brand ambassador.
- *Negotiation:* Master the art of persuasion without pressure. Find win-win solutions that benefit both parties.
- *Networking:* Building a robust professional network opens doors to opportunities you might never have anticipated. My network of historians, linguists, editors and other domain experts has been invaluable for my writing—just as a salesperson's network can lead to unexpected deals.

- *Customer service:* Exceptional service ensures that customers return—and recommend you to others. I answer reader emails personally for this very reason.

Professional Competencies

- *Strategic planning:* A structured approach to sales helps maximise efficiency and results, much like outlining helps me organise complex plots.
- *Market understanding:* Knowing industry trends and customer behaviour ensures your pitches are relevant.
- *Goal orientation:* Clear, measurable goals lead to focus and achievement. I set word count targets daily, which helps me finish a book on time. Revenue targets for salespeople do the same job.
- *Tech-savviness:* Sales has gone digital. Mastering tools like CRM systems and data analytics gives you an edge. I've embraced digital research tools myself over the years.

Self-Assessment: Are You Cut Out for Sales?

Now, let's get personal. Answer the following thirty questions honestly—simple yes or no answers are enough. No cheating—there's no Chanakya here to help you strategise your responses.

1. Do you find people genuinely interesting, and do you enjoy learning what makes them tick?
2. Are you comfortable starting conversations with strangers?

3. Can you explain things to others in a way they understand easily?
4. Do you like helping others figure out what's right for them?
5. Do you feel comfortable asking for things—even if the answer might be no?
6. Do you make an effort to remember small details people share with you?
7. Do you listen carefully and empathise when someone shares a problem?
8. Are you good at picking up on what someone really feels—even if they don't say it?
9. Do you try to understand why someone is upset before reacting?
10. Are you able to find the middle ground when people have different opinions?
11. Can you stay calm when someone is rude or difficult?
12. Do you stay accountable to others when working as part of a team?
13. Do you reach out to friends, family or acquaintances on their birthdays or special occasions?
14. Do you enjoy learning about new things—even if no one asks you to?
15. Do you take courses, read books or watch videos to improve yourself?
16. Do you take feedback seriously, even when it stings a bit?

17. Do you push yourself to stay motivated when things get tough?
18. Do you bounce back quickly after hearing a 'no'?
19. Do you keep going even when something gets boring or repetitive?
20. Are you fine with stepping outside your comfort zone if needed?
21. Do you write down goals or things you want to achieve?
22. Do you plan your day or week ahead of time?
23. Do you follow through on things without being reminded—or maintain a to-do list?
24. Do you take pride in doing things thoroughly, methodically and with attention to detail?
25. When plans go wrong, are you usually the one who finds a fix?
26. Are you OK figuring things out even when the situation is unclear or messy?
27. Do you follow up when someone hasn't replied, but without being pushy?
28. Do you follow up or act on work ideas even outside regular hours—because you want to?
29. Do you feel responsible when something goes wrong—even if it's not fully your fault?
30. Do you use digital tools or apps to stay organised?

How to Interpret Your Answers

Mostly 'Yes'

Well, look at you! You're well-suited for a career in sales. Dive in like I plunge into researching ancient civilisations!

Some 'No'

You may need to develop certain skills, but a career in sales is still within reach. Think of it as a manuscript that needs editing—the foundation exists, but some work is required.

Mostly 'No'

Sales might not align with your strengths right now, but personal growth can change that. Remember, I was a businessman before becoming an author. Transformations *do* happen!

Ashwin's Take, Straight from the Heart

Sales isn't just a career; it's a journey of continuous growth and self-discovery. The most successful salespeople I've met don't simply focus on numbers; they also pay attention to relationships, learning and delivering value—much like authors who don't just count book sales but cherish reader reviews and relationships.

If you've ever wondered whether sales is the right fit for you, remember that skills can be developed, and traits can be nurtured. What matters is your willingness to grow. So, reflect honestly, invest in self-improvement and don't be afraid to take the plunge. After all, every master salesperson started as a curious beginner—just as every bestselling author (including me) began with a blank page and an idea.

As legendary salesperson Zig Ziglar said: 'You don't have to be great to start, but you have to start to be great.' I couldn't have phrased it better myself.

Ready to start your sales journey? The world awaits your pitch, and, who knows, maybe someday I'll be writing about your success story in my next book!